P9-DTI-639

VICTORIAN LUNATICS

VICTORIAN LUNATICS

*A Social Epidemiology of Mental Illness
in Mid-Nineteenth-Century England*

Marlene A. Arieno

Selinsgrove: Susquehanna University Press
London and Toronto: Associated University Presses

Associated University Presses
440 Forsgate Drive
Cranbury, NJ 08512

Associated University Presses
25 Sicilian Avenue
London WC1A 2QH, England

Associated University Presses
P.O. Box 488, Port Credit
Mississauga, Ontario
Canada L5G 4M2

Library of Congress Cataloging-in-Publication Data

Arieno, Marlene A. (Marlene Ann)
    Victorian lunatics : a social epidemiology of mental illness in mid-nineteenth century England / Marlene A. Arieno.
     p. cm.
    Bibliography: p.
    Includes index.
    ISBN 0-945636-03-2 (alk. paper)
    1. Psychiatry—Great Britain—History—19th century. 2. Social psychiatry—Great Britain—History—19th century. I. Title.
RC450.G7A84 1989
616.89'00941—dc19   88-43163
                                        CIP

CONTENTS

FIGURES

TABLES

VICTORIAN LUNATICS

1

INTRODUCTION

Nineteenth-century England was a society experiencing kaleidoscopic change. Charles Dickens's Mr. Gradgrind complained, "By the time I begin to understand and feel half-way comfortable with yesterday, it's already three days beyond tomorrow!" Victorian society's unprecedented increase in population, industrial capacity, and urban growth resulted in massive social change and dislocation. Among the consequences was the national government's determination to respond to the changing face of the society through governmental investigation, regulation, and intervention. One startling social phenomenon of the century was the continuing rise in the proportion of the population officially recognized as insane and the central government's reaction to this originally local responsibility.

In 1807, according to a report of a Parliamentary Select Committee, the incidence of insanity was 2.26 cases in every 10,000 of the general population;[1] by 1844 the number of insane had risen to 12.66 cases per 10,000,[2] an almost sixfold increase. By 1890 the number of madmen per 10,000 increased to 29.63.[3]

Theories as to why this phenomenon occurred, and who made up the rising number of insane, fall into two general categories. The first focuses mainly on the phenomenon itself and claims that societal change generates a social fallout, a percentage of the population that cannot or will not, keep up. The second focuses mainly on the societal response to the rising number of officially recognized insane and explains the phenomenon as a middle-class inspired, governmental scheme of social control. This social control theory, the most prevalent in today's literature, appears to reflect the present fear of contemporary control mechanisms—what we may call the "1984 syndrome."

Both theoretical models, as well as an interest in the phenomenon of insanity itself, have their roots in Michel Foucault's *Madness and Civilization*, which appeared in 1965. Since Foucault burst upon the scene, all writers on the subject have traveled in the wake of his work. The dawn of the Age of Reason was, he argues, a catastrophe for the living metaphors of unreason—the insane.[4] Foucault sees changing perceptions of insanity as the cause of what he calls the "great confinement" that began in the eighteenth century. The imprisonment and degradation of the insane was, to Foucault, the consequence of a shift in the mentality of European society. In the new world of profit and wage labor, madmen became merely another variety of pauper, antagonistic to bourgeois values and perplexing to the authorities. He insists upon the ideological origins of the "great confinement," as he calls the rise of institutionalization. Foucault, however, addressed the general concept of insanity and was little concerned with the precise identity of the insane. The major weakness of his work is that abstractions confront abstractions and the delineation of his theory is often vague. He does not answer various questions raised by the theory of changing perceptions: Whose perceptions changed? Who were the insane? Why was the existence of insanity perplexing to authority? Why was institutionalization seen as the remedy? Foucault simply, although in a very complex style, states that society was given sufficient impetus to implement mass incarceration of the insane because it perceived itself threatened by the mere existence of unreasonable persons coexisting with rational society in the Age of Reason.

After Foucault stimulated the curiosity of the intellectual community, many attempted to develop his work and investigate some of the questions that his theory raised. In 1968, George Rosen, like Foucault, focused mainly on the phenomenon of insanity.[5] He claimed that societal change generates a social fallout of insanity. Rosen suggests that from the eighteenth century onward the concept existed that social stress is related to the causation of mental illness. He suggests the idea that "psychic epidemics" and historical change go hand in hand; society determines mental disorder.[6]

> The history of psychic epidemics is the history of disturbances which the civilization of mankind has experienced. Its changes show us with powerful strokes the turning points at which civilization moves off in new directions. Every true cultural revolution is followed by epidemics, because a large part of the people only gradually enter into the new cultural movement and begin to enjoy its blessings.[7]

By contrast the social control theorists mainly address the societal and governmental response to the seemingly rising numbers of insane. They explain the phenomenon as a middle-class inspired, professional or governmental scheme of social control. Again, accepting Foucault's theory as fact, they attempt to carry it further and answer some of the pragmatic questions raised by that theory. For example, they have elaborately developed explanations of why institutionalization became the accepted remedy to the problem. Thomas Szasz, one of the most prominent social control theorists, singles out the medical profession as the chief conspirator in the "invention" of mental illness. Szasz, in a book that appeared in 1970, *The Manufacture of Madness*,[8] contends that the unusual, eccentric, or unwanted in society have been victims of social control throughout history. Just as Foucault sees the madman as replacing the leper, Szasz sees the madman replacing the witch as a symbol for social deviance. Szasz contends that as "the great ideological conversion from theology to science" took place, society "redefined sin as sickness, and moral sanction as medical treatment."[9] He suggests that the medical profession—in particular, psychiatry—"invented" mental illness to provide itself with a professional market:

> To maintain that a social institution suffers from certain "abuses" is to imply that it has certain other desirable or good uses. This, in my opinion, has been the fatal weakness of the countless exposés—old and recent, literary and professional—of private and public mental hospitals. *My thesis* is quite different; simply put, it is that there are, and can be, no abuses of Institutional Psychiatry, because Institutional Psychiatry is, itself, an abuse.[10]

In 1979, Andrew Scull combined these previous works in a flamboyant book, *Museums of Madness*.[11] His stated purpose is

> to establish how and why insanity came to be exclusively defined as an illness, a condition within the sole jurisdiction of the medical profession; to answer the related question of why the mad-doctors and their reformist mentors opted for the asylum as the domain within which the insane were to receive their "treatment."[12]

Scull accepts, uncritically, Foucault's abstract thesis of "changing perceptions of insanity" without defining the "change" or the "perception." He accepts unconditionally Szasz's thesis that the medical profession "invented" mental illness and defined it further to come under its sole jurisdiction. Scull picks up Rosen's ambiguous suggestion that public order was threatened by the presence of insanity and takes the idea a step further by suggesting that mass incarceration of the insane was a conspiracy between the central government and the medical profession, sanctioned by society's middle class. He contends that the nine-teenth-century reformers were representative of this middle-class conspiracy to remove deviants from society's view. He concedes that "the reformers professed to be actuated by 'humane' concern with the well-being of the lunatic," and proceeds to state that he has "yet to meet a reformer who conceded that his designs on the objects of his attentions were malevolent."[13]

It seems obvious at the outset, then, that Scull approached his subject with a strong bias. His attempt to delineate the effects of the choice of "the asylum as the domain within which the insane were to receive their treatment"[14] amounts to undocumented (and strictly declarative) statements such as:

> Very early on in the history of the asylum, it became apparent that its primary value to the community was as a handy dumping ground to which to consign the awkward and unwanted, the useless and poten-tially troublesome. . . . From the moment the asylums opened, they functioned as museums for the collection of the unwanted.[15]

Scull's thesis is based largely on his unconditional acceptance of the theses previously discussed here and on two tables of aggre-gate statistics showing a rise in the number of officially recognized insane and the rise in pauper versus private patients. His concept of social control asserts simply that "deviants" were identified and subsequently removed from society because of a collusion be-tween the middle class, including its subgroup the medical pro-fession, and the servant of the middle class, the central government. Superficially attractive in its compactness and "anti-establishment" thrust, this view, nevertheless, is grossly over-simplified and neglects empirical validation.

The present study, a modest contribution to the speculations about the place of the insane and the growth of the asylum begun by Foucault, his two aims: it subjects the airy theorizations of the social control advocates to the test of statistical analysis; and it offers an alternative theory to the phenomenon, an interpretation rooted in the bureaucratic revolution of nineteenth-century En-gland.

This study deals not with the abstract concept of insanity but with the product of that abstraction, the insane. Its focus is epi-demiological; it is neither an etiological study (except to give an alternative theory to social control), nor a study of the treatment of the insane. It will be argued that the phenomenon of the in-

creased numbers of officially recognized and subsequently institutionalized insane can be explained, at least in part, as one
result of the changing social values, pervasive in nineteenth-
century England, that led to increased bureaucratization of the
social service delivery system. Further, statistical analysis will
show that Scull's "awkward and unwanted, . . . useless and potentially troublesome" do not constitute the great increase in the
institutionalized. Rather, the statistics suggest quite the opposite;
the institutionalized very closely parallel the general population
with regard to age, sex, and social class.

This study focuses on the period from 1845 to 1862. Two basic
pieces of parliamentary legislation constitute its boundaries. The
first, the Lunatics Act of 1845, made the provision of a county
asylum for pauper lunatics mandatory. The second, an "Act to
amend the Law Relating to Lunatics," was passed in 1862. This
latter measure consolidated much previous legislation, made
provision for voluntary confinement, and required that the cost of
maintenance of pauper lunatics in county asylums, licensed
houses, and registered hospitals be transferred from the funds of
individual parishes to a common Union fund. This act also encouraged the removal of chronic lunatics from their parishes to
the county asylums, thereby increasing county inmate numbers
substantially. Both acts resulted in large numbers of insane being
moved from workhouses to asylums, thus swelling the numbers
of officially recognized lunatics.

The statistical data for this study were compiled from more than
two thousand individual admission records obtained directly
from Bethlehem Hospital, London; Essex County Asylum, Colchester; and Haydock Lodge Asylum, Lancashire, for a distribution of years within the established 1845–62 time frame. The
records of these particular institutions were selected because they
represent the major types of asylums in operation in mid-nineteenth-century England. In mid-century Britain, three distinct
types of institutions existed for the care of the mentally ill: private
asylums (run for profit),[16] county asylums (run with public
funds),[17] and registered hospitals (supported, in full or part, by
voluntary contributions).[18] The three asylums chosen for this
study are representative of these three categories.

Haydock Lodge, a private asylum, was located near the town of
Newton in South Lancashire midway between Liverpool and
Manchester on the railway line connecting these cities and close
to the point where the London and Northwestern Line formed a
junction. Its strategic location made it accessible from almost

every part of the kingdom. The institution, originally a private mansion, had been leased by the government and used as a troop barracks in the early part of the century. In 1843 one George Coode entered into a long-term lease on the mansion, outbuildings, park, and farm for the purpose of adapting the premises to a private lunatic asylum. His sister became the licensed proprietor of the asylum in 1844 when it was authorized by the government to house 40 private (individually paid) and 160 pauper (goverment paid) patients. By 1845, its inmate allowance had already increased to an aggregate of 450, of whom only 50 could, by law, be private patients.[19]

Essex County Asylum, located in Colchester, is representative of the type of asylum established by the 1845 act. During the Easter session of the Essex County Court in 1846, fifteen Justices of the County were elected and subsequently appointed as a committee to supervise the erection of an asylum for pauper lunatics, this in accordance with the Lunatics Act of 1845. In 1847, the boroughs of Colchester and Maldon were united with the county in the effort to provide such an institution. The same year the committee advertised for a building site. "From amongst twelve sites that were offered to them, the Committee, after many enquiries, and after having ascertained that the springs upon the property furnished an ample supply of good water, finally selected the ground on which the asylum has since been erected— 86 acres of the Brentwood Hall Estate."[20] Early in 1853, after a prolonged and careful search, a Dr. Campbell was appointed as medical superintendent, and in September of that year, Essex County Asylum admitted 182 patients; by the end of the year patients numbered 274.[21] For the years 1854 to 1862, 996 individual admission records were selected to be included in the data base for this study.

Bethlehem Hospital, by far the best known of the registered hospitals, was founded in 1247 on land now covered by the Liverpool Street station in London. It originated as a priory attached to the Church of St. Mary of Bethlehem. The current name, "Bethlem," with its innumerable variants of which the most notorious is "Bedlam," is a corruption of Bethlehem, and came into use early in the priory's history.[22]

The hospital's development over its first century is obscure, but it apparently did not prosper, and in 1346 the master and brethren were obliged to petition the city for financial help. As a result it was placed under the supervision of members of the Court of Aldermen, and its association with this body of governors thus precedes the arrangement made by Henry VIII in 1547, giving it to the City of London as a hospital for poor lunatics.[23] It remained under the jurisdiction of the city until 1853, when it was placed under the jurisdiction of the commissioners in lunacy as a registered hospital.

By the late fourteenth century its function as a hospital was established and by 1403 six of the male patients residing there were described as "deprived of their reason."[24] From that time on, Bethlem's ministrations to the mentally ill have continued unbroken. Until the eighteenth century it was the only public institution of its kind in the country. A stipulation of admission was made that the patient be unable to pay for services and that his condition be considered curable. In the eighteenth century a fund was set up for incurable cases, largely supported by a private estate specifically for this purpose. From this point on, Bethlem's status fell somewhere between a public institution and a voluntary, registered hospital.[25]

In 1852 the first resident medical superintendent, Sir Charles Hood, was appointed. Hood initiated an organized system of lectures and clinical instruction, which quickly led to the rise of Bethlem's reputation as a teaching center. Until this time the pauper class formed a large proportion of the asylum's admissions, largely due to the fifteenth-century stipulation that the patient be unable to pay. However, due to the increase in the number of county asylums after the 1845 act and their availability to absorb many of the pauper patients, middle-class patients began to be admitted. "The possession of means, rather than the lack of them, would no longer preclude the opportunity to obtain the best possible treatment available."[26] By midcentury Bethlem Asylum obtained its revenue from a combination of charitable donations and government funds, and it was open to all social classes. Housing 396 patients in 1850, it was typical of a registered metropolitan institution for the insane.[27] A total of 861 case histories were sampled from the admission records of Bethlem Hospital for the years 1845 to 1862 and were included in the data base for the statistical portion of this study.

These admission records—2,005 total from all sampled asylums, the statistical base for this epidemiological study—provide insight into the characteristics of the inmate population of midcentury English asylums.

These records also provide a method of statistically checking the social control theorists' contention that the "unwanted of society" made up the major proportion of asylum inmates. Scull insists the "unwanted" (i.e., those not useful in the market economy of mature capitalism) made up the asylum population. As suggested earlier, however, statistical analysis of these admission records by reference to such categories as age, sex, and prior occupation shows that almost the exact opposite is the case. If we use Scull's definition, the "unwanted" absolutely do not appear in the greater proportion of the asylum population.

The question of the "rising numbers of officially recognized insane"—addressed by all of the theorists, beginning with Foucault—will be taken up in this study as well. "The great confinement," as Foucault terms the rise in the institutionalized insane, was begun in the eighteenth century and continued during the nineteenth century. The idea of changing perceptions of insanity as a cause of this rise in numbers, promoted by Foucault, requires a great leap of faith. Although Foucault did not substantiate his concept that an awareness of humanity's reasonableness caused an increased intolerance of unreason (insanity), it is accepted unquestioningly by those writing in his image. The increase in the number of institutionalized insane is used, by all of these theorists, as both the thematic problem and the proof of the theory. This study will suggest an alternate approach.

It appears more likely that a change in the psychological paradigm, an applied technological advance in biology, resulted in an assumed potential for cure. This perceived cure potential inspired a bureaucracy, oriented toward problem solving, to take action. Asylum development fitted into the general bureaucratic growth of the era, resulting in increased availability of institutional space. Available space allowed increased identification and an available alternative to the traditional methods of dealing with lunacy. Perceptions of insanity did not change, rather a previously unrecognized cure potential appeared and was applied. An in-depth discussion of this critically important change in the psychological paradigm appears in chapter 4 of this study.

Szasz's theory of imperialistic medicine as an explanation of the rising numbers of insane also does not stand the test of historical research. As discussed in chapter 3, the medical profession was so disorganized until well past midcentury that it would have been impossible for the professionals to accomplish any coherent plotting.

Social control, hinted at by Rosen and fully developed by Scull, also is not a solution to this thematic problem. This theory does not stand up to the scrutiny of statistical specificity, as will be seen in chapter 5. This chapter will also explore the role of the "reformer" as a tool of the bourgeoisie, an idea originally suggested by Scull.

Chapter 6 will present and evaluate the alternate theory of general growth of central bureaucracy; it will suggest that no special explanation is needed, but rather that lunacy reform and legislation fit into the general model of "revolution of government." It will show that nineteenth-century England experienced a profound change in the way society perceived itself. An almost religious view of "progress" as the salvation of mankind was pervasive. Industrial innovation and growth and a marked increase in material prosperity had given the Victorians reason to believe that progress and growth were inexorable, leading society to a higher plane of civilization. A spirit of reform accompanied this optimism; a feeling that what could be done, should be done. An enlarged economy provided the financial base from which a multitude of services could be delivered to an expectant populace. However, a delivery system had to be developed to coordinate the effort; into this void stepped governmental bureaucracy. Localism gave way to centralization in the attempt to standardize the distribution of the benefits that a wealthy society could confer upon its members.

However, before entering this historiographical maelstrom, a basic summary of the development of the asylum and its place within the British social service system generally must be attempted in order to provide a basic matrix for the study.

2

DEVELOPMENT OF THE ASYLUM

Within the Social Service Delivery System

> Many political writers . . . have declared that the business of
> government is simply to afford protection, to repel or to
> punish internal or external violence or fraud, and that to do
> more is usurpation. This proposition I cannot admit. The only
> rational foundation of government, the only foundation of a
> right to govern and of a correlative duty to obey, is expedi-
> ency—the general benefit of the community. It is the duty of
> government to do whatever is conducive to the welfare of the
> governed.
>
> —Nassua Senior, 1847

The asylum developed within a social-service delivery system
designed to benefit the inhabitants of England. Although some
private initiatives such as monastic, charitable institutions, like
Bethlem Hospital, existed as early as the thirteenth century, the
history of the development of the formal (governmental) social-
service delivery system, and in particular the asylum, began with
the Poor Law of 1601. Social welfare did not begin with this law;
an informal system of social services existed under feudalism and
later by way of the church and other religiously inspired phi-
lanthropies. Under feudalism there was, at least in theory, no
uncared for distress. In lieu of their freedom, serfs or villeins were
presumed to be protected by their masters from the most acute
sufferings of unemployment, sickness, incapacity, and old age.
When feudalism ceased to be a viable avenue for the alleviation of
need, the church offered one path of organized help for the
person in distress. Christian thought, with its emphasis on the
relief of distress, gave poverty a kind of dignity and made the
granting of alms a meritorious deed. The church was responsible
for economic relief, both in reality and in the popular imagination;
it was, consequently, easy for the government to allow this situation to exist undisturbed. Only in the presence of the overwhelming effects of great social change, when the church could no

20

longer relieve the vastly increased economic need, was public provision introduced, supported by funds secured through taxation.

Positive government action with regard to the relief of the poor and incapacitated began during the reign of Henry VIII. The first statute was enacted in 1531 to address the problems of beggary and vagabondage. The act stated that mayors, justices of the peace, and other local officials should make a diligent search for all "aged, poor and impotent persons" who were compelled to live by alms or the charity of others.[1] The officials should then, according to the act, register them, set geographic limits to areas in which they could beg, and "make and deliver to every such impotent person a letter containing their name, the limit within which he is appointed to beg and witness that he is authorized to beg."[2] Although this act did not directly respond to the plight of the needy, it did represent to some degree the assumption by government of responsibility for the care of persons economically distressed. It was a beginning.

The act went on to impose fines on those who would give money or lodging to "any beggar being strong and able in their bodies to work."[3] Any beggar or vagabond found idle was to be "enjoined upon his oath to return forthwith to the place where he was born, and there put himself to labour like a true man oweth to do."[4]

As early as 1536, it became apparent that something more was needed; therefore, the following stipulations were added to the statute of 1531: children between the ages of five and fourteen, who are begging or idle, shall be apprenticed to craft masters; preachers shall exhort their flocks to be charitable to the poor and said contributions shall be accounted for by the collectors; and rich parishes shall distribute their surplus to poorer parishes for sustenance.[5] Here all the elements of the Poor Law of 1601 were prefigured. In place of the system of begging, allowed for in 1531, an administration of funds was substituted and supplied through contributions, by a combination of government and church. The act also stipulated that the funds collected be accounted for, thereby making record keeping mandatory. Embryonic administrative machinery was taking shape.

By 1563, the exhortations to contribute gave way to social pressure, and gentle persuasion was backed up by the legal power of the justices to "sesse, tax and limit upon every obstinate person a weekly sum to be paid toward the relief of the poor."[6] If the "obstinate person" refused the assessment, a prison term awaited him. With this statute the move from voluntary to compulsory granting of alms was effected.

The short step to taxation was taken in 1572 with the passage of the 14th Elizabeth. The principles of the previous statutes were maintained, but a radically new, critically important provision was added. The justices of the peace and other local officials

> shall by their good discretions tax and assess all and every inhabitant dwelling in all and every city, borough, town, village, hamlet and place . . . to such weekly charge as they and every of them shall weekly contribute towards the relief of the said poor people and the names of all such inhabitants taxed shall also enter into the said register book together with their taxation.[7]

An amendment in 1576 mandated that "poor and needy persons being willing to work may be set on work."[8] Wool, hemp, and flax were provided to such able-bodied persons, which when made into yarn or rope, was collected by a government official and sold. A portion of the proceeds was paid to the worker. A further stipulation was made in case of a refusal on the part of the able-bodied to comply:

> If hereafter any such person able to do any such work shall refuse to work or shall go abroad begging or live idly, or taking such work shall spoil or embezzle the same, then in convenient apparel meet for such a body to wear he shall be received into such House of Correction there to be straightly kept, as well in diet as in work, and also punished from time to time.[9]

Government-sponsored work programs were added to taxation, not merely for punitive purposes, but to increase the revenue required for the poor relief delivery system.

Economic hard times in 1596–97—a period of actual starvation—fostered another addition to the growing body of poor-relief legislation. The Act of 1598 consolidated and clarified the programs of 1572 and 1576, and added a provision for the erection of "working houses and hospitals for the poor . . . convenient houses of habitation for the lame, impotent, old and blind."[10] The intent was to alleviate the current famine conditions. The funding was to come from a tax levied on every parish inhabitant and every occupier of land. The local justices were empowered to fix the rate of assessment. With the passage of this 1598 addendum, the stage was set for the Poor Law Act of 1601, the culminating statute in the development of governmental responsibility of poor relief.

The Elizabethan Poor Law Act of 1601 was epoch making; the actual administration of it was carried out locally, but the act itself was countrywide in scope. The universality of the law, which made it a milestone in the development of a social-service delivery system, came about in response to a universal need and demand on the part of the populace. These demands could only be relieved by the application of public resources to individual need. Formal recognition of every man's responsibility for every man's distress was established in the 43rd Elizabeth.[11]

Thus we see that in 1531 the aged, poor, and impotent were "allowed" to beg. By 1536, contributions were elicited for the relief of the needy. In 1563 the exhortations to contribute gave way to a compulsory giving of relief to the needy; 1572 saw an embryonic system of taxation administered by local justices. In 1576, government-sponsored work programs for the able-bodied poor were added to the previous legislation to increase revenue needed for poor relief. A 1598 act consolidated the 1572 and 1576 acts and added the workhouse concept to the relief system. The 1601 Elizabethan Poor Law Act was a culmination of the process of applying public resources to individual need according to central-government decree.

The purpose of delineating this process is not to familiarize the reader with isolated acts relating to the early system of poor relief, but rather to establish that the precedent of central-government intervention into the process was set in the sixteenth century. The theory of centralization of bureaucracy and government responsibility for the insane poor in the nineteenth century will be presented as an alternate theory to social control of the poor.

During the years chronicled so far, the insane were lumped in with other needy persons who were incompetent to care for themselves. They were at first allowed to beg, later allowed to receive charity, subsequently allowed to work, if possible, and eventually incarcerated in workhouses and hospitals, if they were unable or unwilling to work. Throughout this period many remained outside the jurisdiction of government regulation. Some were cared for by their families, others were housed in private madhouses, and the remainder limped along through life unhelped and unharmed.

Foucault has characterized the eighteenth century as the period of "great confinement"—a period when society chose the lunatic to fill the social position of exclusion once filled by the leper. Although he fails to make this thesis believable, the eighteenth century did see the first official recognition of the insane in an English statute. The 12th Anne, in 1714, distinguished for the first time between impoverished lunatics and rogues, vagabonds, beggars, and vagrants.[12] The act allowed for the apprehension of dangerous lunatics by town or parish officials and their subsequent detention, the cost of which was to be paid by the parish of the lunatic's legal settlement. The Vagrant's Act of 1744 added the cost of "cure" for the lunatic to the cost of detention to be paid by his home parish.[13] The "cure" often took place in private boarding houses, which gradually acquired the name of "madhouses."

William Parry-Jones, in *The Trade in Lunacy*,[14] describes several such eighteenth-century private madhouses that housed pauper lunatics at parish expense. One of the earliest of these private houses was Hook Norton, established in 1725 and described in a notice for its sale by auction in 1778:

> A freehold convenient house, fitted in a most excellent manner for the reception of lunaticks. Upon the ground floor, kitchen, parlour, apothecary's shop, wood-house and stable, and a garden thereto adjoining a back-yard with a large pair of gates and is fit for a surgeon or apothecary.[15]

In 1744 the Henley-in-Arden madhouse was licensed in Warwickshire, and Fishponds madhouse, near Bristol in Gloucestershire, dates from 1760. In 1770 such residences were reported to exist in Horningsham and Wiltshire, and Ricehurst Asylum in Sussex was licensed in 1792. In the London area, three private asylums date from the mid-eighteenth century: Brooke House, Clapton; Beaufort House, Fulman; and Whitmore House, Huxton.

The private madhouse system, however, was subjected to persistent disparagement and censure. The basic flaw, around which alleged defects were centered, was the "principle of profit" on which the system was founded. In 1706, Daniel Defoe stimulated public interest in the subject through a pamphlet that alleged the wrongful detention of a young woman in a private asylum.[16] This pamphlet began the publication of many such articles reflecting public concern about the practices of the private madhouse system. Consequently, in 1754, the College of Physicians of London was asked to consider a bill recommending that the college take the responsibility for the licensing and inspection of these private asylums; the college rejected the proposal as too "inconvenient" to undertake.

After the College of Physicians declined the proposal, evidence of abuses continued to accumulate, and finally led to a Select Committee inquiry in 1763. After considerable investigation, the committee's report concluded that legislation was in order. In 1774, the first act for the regulation of private madhouses was enacted. It provided for

> the licensing and inspection of private madhouses within the cities of London and Westminster and within a radius of seven miles thereof; five Commissioners appointed by the College of Physicians shall accomplish the task. Throughout the rest of England and Wales, licensing and inspection shall be carried out by the justices of the peace accompanied by a medical practitioner. A medical certificate confirming insanity shall be required before confinement of non-pauper patients can take place.[17]

The act was made perpetual in 1786.[18]

By the end of the eighteenth century, it became apparent that the private sector could not adequately fill the need for supervision and care of the insane. The supply of space in private houses far outdistanced the demand for care. The public sector was doing little toward filling this need except providing space in workhouses. At this time, the founding of voluntary public-subscription institutions began in an attempt to fill the void. These hospitals, however, provided little relief for the increasing number of insane poor.

Alarm about the apparent increase in the incidence of insanity and the failure of the asylum system to provide adequate facilities led to the appointment of a Select Committee of the House of Commons in 1807 charged with investigating the state of criminal and pauper lunatics in England and Wales. The efforts of Sir George Paul, a Gloucestershire magistrate, who urged the establishment of a system of tax-supported asylums for the "relief and comfort" of lunatics were paramount in bringing about the investigation. The committee observed that the treatment of pauper lunatics boarded in private madhouses depended "wholly upon the good conduct of the Keeper."[19] J. W. Rogers, a former apothecary, described, in a pamphlet, atrocities perpetrated in the private houses which included "prolonged restraint, theft and misuse of the patient's personal belongings and clothing, beating, whipping, raping of married and single women, inhumane procedures, such as the 'mopping-down' of incontinent patients under an outside pump and the brutal use of instruments."[20]

Although it is difficult to ascertain the validity of Rogers' statements, as he was accused of deliberate falsification of the facts concerning Warburton asylum because of a personal grudge he held against its owner and operator, testimony given before the 1807 committee suggested that abuses did in fact take place in private madhouses. The committee's report suggested that "the measure which appears most adequate to enforce the proper care and management of these unfortunate persons and the most likely to conduce to their perfect cure, is the erection of Asylums for their reception in the different parts of the kingdom."[21] A plan was outlined for the erection of sixteen asylums, each to care for up to three hundred lunatics, and each serving a district containing a population of approximately half a million.[22]

The Report of 1807 led directly to the County Asylum Act of 1808,[23] which recommended that the magistrates of a single county, or group of counties, be allowed to authorize the erection of an asylum, the cost of which would be paid by county rates. The cost of maintaining pauper lunatics would come from their native parishes. Few counties were able to comply with the recommendations because of financial constraints. The act was amended in 1815 allowing counties to borrow the money for a period of fourteen years in order to establish asylums,[24] but the progress of the movement remained slow. By 1824 only nine counties had responded.[25]

In 1828 the Madhouse Act was passed,[26] providing for the establishment of a new commission to license and oversee asylums. Its activities, however, were to be confined to the metropolitan area of London. The metropolitan commissioners numbered fifteen and included five general practitioners who replaced the five Fellows of the College of Physicians provided for in the 1744 act. Their authority was limited to private metropolitan asylums, leaving the magistrates to fulfill these duties in the provinces. County and public hospitals or asylums were exempted. This Metropolitan Commission on Lunacy remained in the forefront of the reform movement. It proved to be an extremely effective pressure group and was instrumental in revising and extending the reform of 1828.

Prior to the nineteenth century, progress in the movement to aid those in need of relief—particularly, the insane—remained limited. The art of public administration had not yet reached a point where it was effective, and the thought of the times did not really contemplate government in that role. In organization, method, and personnel, the administration of relief in the seventeen and eighteenth centuries had not developed to a point at which it could provide any degree of effectiveness; the unit of operation was too small. Local government did not possess adequate resources to assume such responsibilities. In 1834, the year of the New Poor Law, the population of England was fourteen million and there existed fifteen thousand parishes, an average of less than one thousand persons to a parish.[27]

The 1834 reform of the Poor Law contained two basic provisions.[28] First, it denied outdoor relief to the able-bodied poor and defined the workhouse as the mechanism through which the policy would be carried out. Second, and for our purposes the more important, it centralized the administration of relief by creating larger units of operation. The latter provided for an appointed central board to be responsible for Poor Law administration with assistant commissioners empowered to frame and enforce regulations to govern the running of workhouses. All regulations were to be uniform throughout the country.[29] After more than two hundred years of the most extreme form of localism, England was moving toward national supervision and larger administrative units. Within three years, 13,264 parishes, 90 percent of the number to which the law in this particular act applied, had formed themselves into 568 unions.[30] Administrative centralization had progressed to the point at which asylum reform could effectively take place.

The 1834 act, while establishing the administrative machinery appropriate to tackling the lunacy problem with government-sponsored asylums, also created an alternative solution—the workhouse. Although the 47th Clause of the Poor Law Amendment Act stated that "lunatics and idiots" were not to be detained in workhouses for longer than fourteen days, the law was quite commonly ignored, except in the case of dangerous lunatics. The reason was the difference in the cost of maintenance of the pauper lunatic to his native parish. The cost of boarding out one lunatic in a private asylum was ten to twelve shillings per week, whereas the workhouse cost half that amount.[31] That the workhouse was not the "best care" for the insane was detailed in the First Annual Report of the Poor Law Commission:

The workhouse was filthy in the extreme, the appearance of the inmates dirty and wretched. In one corner of the building was the most filthy, dismal-looking room which upon entering became almost impossible to forget. The sole tenant of this abode was a poor distressed lunatic. His appearance was pitiable in the extreme; his clothing was extremely ragged; his flesh literally as dirty as the floor; his head and face were much bruised, apparently from repeated falls. Shoes he had been furnished with at some time or other, but they had done their duty, and his feet protruded through them. He sat listless and alone, without any human being to attend upon or take care of him, staring vacantly around, insensible even to the calls of nature. To the great shame of the parish officers, he had been in this disgusting state for years.[32]

The assistant commissioner, Charles Mott, also reported that the appearance of many of the inmates in the old workhouses indicated a state of insanity, but governors maintained they were harmless. Even when they were perceived dangerous by the other inmates, the governors refused to send them to an asylum because of the expense. The detention of lunatics in the workhouses occurred mostly in the provinces; in London lunatics were well provided for because of the surveillance activity of the lunacy commissioners.[33]

Evidence was also given before the Select Committee of 1838 on the scandalous conditions endured by destitute lunatics in the workhouses. The commissioners recommended that they or the home secretary should have the power to unite several unions for the purpose of erecting common asylums.[34] But again financial considerations held sway, for the erection of a workhouse cost on an average £40 per person, whereas a county asylum varied from £100 to £350 a head.[35]

The same year, the metropolitan commissioners in their Annual Report also suggested further government intervention.[36] The commissioners stressed the improvements brought about by their assiduous and frequent inspections and contrasted this improvement in the conditions in the metropolis with the stagnation or retrogression in the provinces, where "the salutary provisions of the Act by which it is required that all houses shall be annually licensed and periodically visited and reported on by the Visiting Magistrates, have been in great degree neglected or violated."[37] However, action was not taken on these suggestions until 1842, when Lord Granville Somerset, chairman of the commission, sent a bill to be introduced into the Commons to extend the Metropolitan Commission's powers for three years to allow it to carry out a comprehensive inspection of all asylums and madhouses in the country.[38] The subsequent inspections resulted in 1844 in a comprehensive report detailing the extensive findings of the visitors. The commission found that institutions in several categories were "reasonably satisfactory," but the majority of asylums and licensed houses deserved "unqualified censure."[39] Abuses were widely cited, such as those at a house in Derby:

> The straw in the paupers' beds was found filthy, and some of the bedding was in a disgusting condition from running sores, and was of the worst materials, and insufficient. Two cells, in which three sick epileptic paupers slept, were damp, unhealthy, and unfit for habitation. The beds of some of the private patients were in an equally bad state.[40]

A major theme of the report was that only the creation of a national inspectorate on a permanent basis would eliminate such abuses. The report also revealed that three-quarters of the total number of lunatics were still in workhouses, farmed out, or in private asylums where their condition was often pitiable. Detailed recommendations about the direction that reform should take were presented to both houses of Parliament. Anthony Ashley Cooper (Lord Shaftesbury), a prominent member of the Metropolitan Lunacy Commission, made a speech before the House of Commons in 1845 in which he expressed the views of the lunacy reformers: "Our present business . . . is to affirm that poor lunatics ought to be maintained at the public charge. I entertain a very decided opinion that none of any class should be received for profit; but all, I hope will agree that paupers, at any rate should not be the subjects of financial speculation."[41]

Ashley was eminent among the contemporary lunacy reformers, but in many ways he was representative of them. He personified the conscience of the Victorian age. He perceived himself committed to a cause—at first, that of the factory workers, and later, that of the most helpless and destitute classes of society, the poor and especially the insane poor. Ashley had been a member of the Lunacy Commission since 1828, and from 1829 until the 1845 legislation he was often chairman. He became permanent chairman after the 1845 bills became law and remained so until his death in 1881. No one else was as involved as he in lunacy reform, and when his bill was legislated it was known as "Ashley's Act." Upon introduction of the bills in June 1845, he concluded his speech by begging the Commons to reflect that they were in a sense legislating for themselves. "It is our duty and our interest too when we have health and intellect to deliberate upon these things before the evil days come. Here we are sitting in deliberation today; tomorrow we may be subjects of this fearful affliction. How frail is the tenure by which we hold all that is previous and dignified in human nature."[42] The two bills he proposed both received government backing and passed swiftly through both Houses of Parliament, becoming law on the 4th and 8th of August 1845.

The first Lunatics Act of 1845 established a permanent national Lunacy Commission.[43] "The Lord Chancellor is empowered to appoint Two Persons, to be called 'The Commissioners in Lunacy,' and shall henceforth be called 'The Masters in Lunacy,' and shall take the same rank and Precedence as the Masters in Ordinary of the High Court of Chancery."[44] Having established the positions of "Masters in Lunacy," the act goes on to establish a commission and to name the first commissioners. Provision was also made for a secretary of the commission. The jurisdiction in which the commissioners were empowered to grant licenses for asylums and madhouses was defined:

> The cities of London and Westminster, the County of Middlesex, the Borough of Southward, and several Parishes and Places herein-after mentioned . . . and in the Counties of Surrey, Kent and Essex; and also within every other place within the Distance of Seven Miles from any part of the said Cities of London or Westminster, shall be the immediate jurisdiction of the Commission.[45]

Provision for licensing asylums beyond the immediate jurisdiction of the Lunacy Commission was made in the act by giving the authority to the justices of the peace for the county or borough. However, the justices were accountable to the commission in totality because "within fourteen days after such license shall have been granted, a copy thereof must be sent to the Commissioners for their approval."[46] The act also provided for the type of inspection previously carried out by the metropolitan commissioners. However, the jurisdiction for inspection was now countrywide, and notification of inspection was no longer required:

> Every licensed House shall, without any previous notice, be visited by Two at least of the Commissioners (one of whom shall be a Physician or Surgeon, and the other a Barrister) at least four times in every year, if the house is within the immediate jurisdiction of the Commissioners, and if not, it shall be visited at least twice every year.[47]

On such visits, the commissioners were instructed and empowered to collect data for their reports, which were due annually to the lord chancellor.

The second Lunatics Act of 1845 made the erection of county and borough asylums compulsory.[48]

That the Justices of every County and Borough which has no Asylum for the Pauper Lunatics shall either erect or provide an Asylum for the Pauper Lunatics of such County or Borough alone, or shall unite with some County or Borough in erecting or providing an asylum. If, within the period of three years from the passing of this Act, they have not done so, it shall be lawful for one of Her Majesty's Principal Secretaries of State to require the Justices to do so.[49]

The financing of the county asylums was to come from a general county tax collected by the county treasurer and then turned over to the treasurer of the asylum. Provision was also made for the erection of asylums financed by monies advanced from the central government to the county upon the mortgaging of the tax rates to be collected.[50]

The second act also made it explicit that the lunacy commissioners had the last word about asylum matters:

Every Committee of Visitors shall, within twelve months after the passing of this Act or in the case of every asylum already established, or to be established, submit the existing general rules of the asylum for the approval by Her Majesty's Secretary of State. Upon approval, the rules shall be printed, abided by and observed by the management of the asylum.[51]

The universality of the act is apparent in its scope with regard to the jurisdiction, visitation, financing, and management authority that was given to the central government. No longer was the care of lunatics a local matter.

The pervasiveness of the act was clear. "Every City, Town, Liberty, Parish, Place or District, not being a Borough or part of a Borough, shall for the purposes of this Act, be annexed to and be treated and taxed as part of the Country within which it is situated. This Act shall extend to all of England and Wales."[52] The only exception to the act was Bethlem Hospital, initially exempted because it was deeded to the City of London by Henry VIII. That sixteenth-century deeding was rectified by an amending act in 1853,[53] which placed it under the jurisdiction of the commissioners in lunacy and registered it as a hospital. The term *hospital* was defined as "Any Hospital or part of an Hospital or other House or Institution where Lunatics are received and supported wholly or partly by voluntary contributions or by any charitable bequest or gift or by the application of any excesses of payments of some patients towards the support, provision or benefit of other patients."[54]

The Lunatics Act of 1845, although amended in 1853, remained in substance the controlling legislation regarding lunatics and asylums until very late in the nineteenth century. During the period of this study and beyond, the demand for asylum space far outstripped the supply. The widespread erection of county asylums led to the progressive withdrawal of pauper lunatics from private asylums and workhouses, swelling the numbers of the officially recognized numbers of insane persons. Local agencies, previously unwilling to withdraw lunatics from workhouses because of cost considerations, were in 1845 required to do so by law. They were required to build asylums by central-government insistence, and were less reluctant to do so than in the past because of central-government financing schemes. However, despite careful planning by county officials designed to meet the estimated demands, asylums quickly became overcrowded and additional accommodations had to be built in most asylums.

The era of large-scale institutionalization of the insane was taking shape within the social-service delivery system under the auspices of the central government. The relief of the needy, and in particular the insane, which we have traced from its embryonic stage in the sixteenth century to full-blown institutionalization in the nineteenth century, came as a result of an increased demand that the private sector could not effectively handle.

The phenomenon of the increased numbers of officially recognized and subsequently institutionalized insane can be explained, at least in part, as one result of the changing social values pervasive in nineteenth-century England, which led to increased bureaucratization of the social-service delivery system. A spirit of reform accompanied a spirit of optimism. No particular change in the view of the insane accompanied the spirit of reform; increased social responsibility was shown for all unfortunate persons.

The year 1714 marks the first governmental distinction between lunatics and other improverished people, and in 1774 the concept of care and cure for lunatics became public policy. That year also saw the first legislation regulating the licensing and inspection of madhouses. From that point on, further investigation led to further intervention by the central government. Once care and perceived cure became officially recognized as a societal responsibility, the demand for space exceeded the availability in private institutions. Public expectations and the dedicated work of reformers eventually culminated in the 1845 act. Dating from that act, increased indentification and relocation of lunatics housed in workhouses greatly swelled the numbers of official pauper lunatics. In 1844 the commissioners in lunacy published a report that revealed that nine thousand (three-quarters of all lunatics) were still existing in workhouses.[55] One of the predominant activities of the lunacy commissioners was to get the insane out of the workhouse and into the asylum. It is obvious that the relocation of these workhouse lunatics into the official number tally accounted for a large part of the increase, thereby negating the basic assumption of the social control theorists.

With regard to Scull's assertion that the mad-doctors and their reformist mentors opted for the asylum as a means of creating a place of incarceration for the "unwanted" of society, it has been noted that the asylum held historical precedents. As early as 1547, Henry VIII decreed Bethlem to be set aside for lunatics. During the parliamentary debates held concerning the Madhouse Act of 1828, Mr. F. J. Browne, who had given a manor house to the county of Dorset, along with the funds to maintain it, commented that being as England had been an early leader in the provisions made for the insane, it was time that the country should move in the forefront of reform and regain the lead in that aspect of social welfare. He stated that "the time is fast approaching when England will emulate the example of the continent on the subject. In Holland, in France, in Italy, and even in Spain (meanly as we thought of that country), there are establishments existing for the reception of lunatics at government expense."[56] He concluded by moving for leave to bring in a bill that he said "will consolidate and amend the several acts, respecting County Lunatic Asylums, and facilitate the erection of such asylums to improve the conditions and treatment of Pauper Lunatics."[57]

It can be seen that asylum development was part of the general development of the social service delivery system and generally evolutionary in nature. The nineteenth-century escalation in asylum growth can be viewed as part of the "revolution in government" spurred by the social consciousness of the era. However, before exploring this alternate theory in detail, it is necessary to move to a discussion of the development of the health care system and the state of the medical profession during the period when Szasz suggests that it "invented" mental illness to serve its own purpose.[58]

3

THE DEVELOPMENT OF THE HEALTH-CARE DELIVERY SYSTEM

The Medical Profession

Hospitals are the measure of a civilization.
—Jacques Tenon, Paris, 1788

Prior to the Medical Act of 1858, the medical profession was in a fragmented, chaotic, and unmanageable state of disorganization. Contrary to Thomas Szasz's theory that the medical profession used mental illness to provide itself with a human reserve of experimental specimens as well as a market with which to line its pockets, the profession, as a whole, nearly ignored the subject of insanity. Even if the practitioners had been interested in the phenomenon, the physicians were not in a position to plan a coherent undertaking of that magnitude.

During the parliamentary debates that preceded the 1858 legislation, Walpole summarized the objectives of the proposed bill as: to raise to a uniform and sufficient standard the education and acquirements of all persons who enter the medical profession; to have an authoritative register, clearly defining those who have attained the prescribed qualifications; and to remove all of the local jurisdictions that restrict a competent person from practicing in any other part of the country than that in which the licensing body that passed him had authority.[1] These objectives, which were passed into law, were intended to create order out of the chaos that prevailed in the health care system.

Chairman S. H. Walpole and his committee were conscious of the serious difficulties in meeting the objectives of the proposed bill because the laws under which they had been operating were "inapplicable to the times in which we live." In addition, "the privileges conferred upon the medical degree granting bodies involve many anomalies and absurdities."[2] M. P. Brady, giving testimony in the debate, made the observation again "that great inconvenience arose out of the present system of rivalry between the various medical bodies."[3] Walpole worried that the greatest problem in implementing objectives was the fact that the law-makers "are starting, as it were, at a wrong point."[4] They found the medical profession not in the hands of those who were most competent, but going back to the original state of the law "we find that through the middle ages the matter had got into the hands of the ecclesiastical authorities. Those authorities were unwilling to understand or undertake the surgical part of the profession, but they maintained power and authority over the physicians."[5]

By means of an act of Henry VIII, a medical corporation with powers of exclusive authority within seven miles of St. Paul's in London had been created, while the universities inherited from the ecclesiastical authorities the power of conferring degrees giving the privilege to practice.[6] Another anomaly, according to Walpole, involved "different bodies in different parts of the kingdom having the power to give licenses to practise."[7] They had to contend with the College of Physicians, established in 1511, and the College of Surgeons, the latter more or less connected with the Corporation of Barbers. However, by means of their charter in 1800, the surgeons had obtained the right to grant diplomas. Thus, according to Walpole, "they had an authority vested in the College of Surgeons; but that authority was not an exclusive one which could be enforced in law, like that of the College of Physicians."[8] Further complicating matters was the place of the apothecary in the health-care delivery system.

In England, surgeons were distinct from apothecaries, whereas in Scotland surgeons and apothecaries were more commonly combined. Scotland, in fact, had a totally different set of medical laws, which seriously limited the free flow of practitioners between the countries. A similar situation existed in Ireland.[9] At the same time, in Scotland the universities of Aberdeen and Glasgow had the power to confer degrees valid throughout the whole kingdom, including the capital, because the College of Physicians in Edinburgh did not have that exclusive authority possessed by the College of Physicians in London. The University in Dublin had the same kind of privilege that the universities of Oxford and Cambridge possessed, whereas the newer universities in Ireland were restricted to conferral of degrees that entitled the practitioner to practice in Ireland. Graduates of continental universities also were not entitled to practice in England, although they were allowed to do so in Scotland and Ireland.[10] By these intricate explanations Walpole sought to emphasize the chaotic state of the medical profession.

His remedy for the confusion was straightforward:

> Instead of continuing this anomalous state of things, instead of pre-serving an exclusive privilege in one part of the kingdom to the detriment of another, the public should have the right of calling in such advise as they believed to be the best; and the first great principle that he should submit to the House was that there should be reciproc-ity of practise in all parts of the United Kingdom.[11]

His arguments were convincing and the proposed legislation passed into law in 1858. Until well past midcentury, however, the medical profession was anything but a cohesive unit capable of plotting malicious, self-serving strategies for the incarceration of the insane. Although the chaotic situation of the medical profes-sion in the mid-nineteenth century has been amply described, it is well worth the historical excursion to discern how that state of affairs came to be.

During the medieval period, the development of the medical profession was slow, but the stratification that was apparent in the nineteenth-century parliamentary debates began to take shape. The split in authority that came about when secular bodies took over from ecclesiastical groups persisted well into the nineteenth century and assumed that physicians, surgeons, and apothecaries were separate and mutually exclusive orders. In theory, a physi-cian was a person who possessed a university degree in medicine and who confined his practice to internal medicine. Physicians made a diagnosis, gave a prognosis, and wrote prescriptions for medicine that the apothecaries filled. Surgeons treated patients manually; besides operating, they employed salves, plasters, lini-ments, and lotions, all applied externally as they could not give medicine internally—that being the exclusive domain of the phy-sician. Surgeons and apothecaries were trained through appren-ticeship. Apothecaries dispensed medicines prescribed by physicians as a primary function; however, they also dispensed advice, giving a diagnosis and suggesting the appropriate medi-cine or treatment plan. They were prohibited by law from charg-ing for such advice—that too being the exclusive domain of the physician—so their income was derived from the sale of medicine alone.

Although there was considerable overlapping of functions in practice, in theory and status, the three orders within the medical profession remained quite separate, with each order guarding its special rights and privileges through its own guild. These medieval guilds became, in time, medical corporations that oversaw the education and licensing of their own order. As P. B. Cowper commented during the 1858 debates, "By the common law any person was entitled to practise medicine, provided he was competent, but a number of statutes had been passed from the time of Henry VIII, regulating the bodies entitled to decide the question."[12]

The physician tended to regard himself as an intellectual and was in fact generally regarded as the elite of the medical professionals. His education, generally obtained at Oxford or Cambridge, was literary and theoretical, involving attendance at lectures and disputations on the theory, logic, and practice of medicine. The earliest colleges of Oxford and Cambridge have no exact foundation dates, because they evolved as students gathered around teachers from the monastery schools, but the existence of a medical faculty at Cambridge is evident in 1312 when the first M.D. degree was issued.[13] In 1421 a petition was presented to Parliament by the sister universities requesting that in the future only those with university degrees in medicine be allowed to practice, and that these universities be the examining and licensing bodies.[14] Nothing came of this petition, but in 1511, Henry VIII, an amateur physician himself, instigated the first Medical Act, which made it an offense to practice medicine unless one was a graduate of a university or had been licensed by the bishop in his diocese after examination by a panel of experts.

The 1511 Medical Act helped to formalize medical education and to establish a body of responsibly trained medical men. Although it did little to improve medical training, it did represent a beginning in the professionalization of medical practice. Further progress was made in 1518, when Henry issued a charter establishing a Company of Physicians in London, which became the Royal College of Physicians in 1551.[15] The charter empowered the company to examine and license physicians throughout the kingdom. The Royal College of Physicians expected its members to be graduates of Oxford or Cambridge, which insured that they were all members of the Church of England, and secured economic selectivism as well, because those universities were only available to the upper classes.[16] This kind of professional snobbery was still very apparent in evidence given before an 1834 Select Committee to inquire into the regulations regarding the education and practice of the various branches of the medical profession. Sir Henry

Halford Bart, M.D., while being questioned about the legality of confining the choice of College of Physicians officers to graduates of Oxford and Cambridge, replied "There is a certain preference of those members in the mind of the fellows of the College; for they are the people who have undergone a moral and intellectual trial in the universities from whence they came, to which they are not subject at the foreign or provincial universities."[17]

Modern surgeons evolved from the old medieval barber-surgeons, who had in turn evolved from barbers, and were of a distinctly lower social status than the physicians. The barbers of Dublin, in 1446, were the first to receive a charter. They were followed, in 1462, by the barber-surgeons of London, who were destined to become the most important of the early corporations when, in the nineteenth century, they become the College of Surgeons. The third early barber-surgeons' guild to have an impact on medical education was founded by the town council of Edinburgh in 1505. It was stipulated in the Edinburgh charter that its members were to receive instruction in anatomy, and toward this end the corporation was given a corpse of one of the city's executed criminals annually for dissection. This marks the first attempt at "hands on" medical education in Britain.[18]

Within the next hundred years similar bodies had developed in many of the provincial towns. The guilds of York, Bristol, and Newcastle eventually distinguished themselves by organizing anatomical instruction for barber-surgeons. Many of the provincial guilds, however, never evolved into medical corporations with statutory powers and the majority of them were absorbed into amalgamations of various trading groups, whereas those of Dublin, Edinburgh and London evolved into modern corporations.[19]

In 1540, the king assented to a union of all the barber-surgeon guilds in England. The United Company of Barber-Surgeons' charter stipulated that the surgeon was no longer required to act the part of the barber, while the barbers were ordered to restrict their surgical operations to dentistry. The charter also entitled the company to receive the bodies of four executed criminals each year for the purpose of dissection and the study of anatomy.[20] The barber-surgeons, although still inferior in rank and status to the physicians, were the vanguard of modern clinical medical education. By the nineteenth century, it was they who led the field in anatomical teaching in the hospitals and the special schools of anatomy.[21]

Just as surgeons were compromised by their linkage to barbers, so the apothecaries had a long standing association with grocers.

Confusion arose because apothecaries often sold exotic groceries as well as drugs, and the grocers often included simple drug compounds in their stock of groceries. In 1606, the apothecaries were actually incorporated into the large Grocers' Company as a separate section, so powerful was the grocers' association. This created great consternation among the apothecaries who saw themselves as medical professionals serving the public as general practitioners. There was a great deal of practical truth in their self-perception. For the poor to average-income person, who could not afford a university-educated physician, the apothecary was the only "doctor" available. King James I, who dabbled in pharmacy himself, initiated their separation from the grocers. In 1617 he granted them a charter to become the Society of Apothecaries of the City of London.[22] The charter gave them authorization to supervise their craft and to restrict entry into practice to those who completed a five-year apprenticeship and an examination. The examiner's oath gives an interesting insight into the society's self-perception:

> I do solemnly promise swear (or being one of the people called quakers, so solemnly affirm), that I will faithfully, impartially and honestly, according to the best of my skill and knowledge, execute the trust reposed in me by the master, wardens, and society of the art and mystery of apothecaries of the city of London, as an examiner, in the examination of every person who shall come before me to be examined as to his fitness or qualifications to act as an apothecary, or assistant to an apothecary, as the case may be, and that without favour, affection, prejudice, or malice. So Help Me God.[23]

This oath was included in the Apothecaries Act of 1815 and had not been substantially changed since the time of James I. Once separated from the grocers, the apothecaries continued to serve the public effectively as unofficial general practitioners throughout the seventeenth and eighteenth centuries. Their position and function were finally legitimized by the milestone Apothecary Act in the nineteenth century.[24]

Although all three orders of the medical profession by the early seventeenth century had established corporations with increasing powers to examine and license, or at least supervise, entrance to their crafts, formal education in the medical specialities was not universally encouraged. James VI of Scotland (later James I of England), for example, had relatively enlightened ideas on medical organization, but when in 1599 he established the Faculty of Physicians and Surgeons of Glasgow, no mention was made of education, and the powers granted were only to examine, admit, allow, and approve the entrants.[25] In some cases education was actually discouraged, as in the foundation charter of the Edinburgh College of Physicians in 1681, which stated that the group was prohibited from teaching. The teaching function in Edinburgh was reserved only for the surgeons,[26] who were continuing their interest in the research and teaching of anatomy. In 1697 they successfully petitioned the town council to build a new anatomy theater and by 1705 regular anatomy classes were held for barber-surgeon apprentices; the town council also agreed at that time to pay the instructor's salary.[27] The same sort of development took place in Glasgow where the barber-surgeons undertook the teaching of anatomy, while the University Faculty of Physicians remained a mere licensing body.[28]

The University of Edinburgh, founded in 1583, eventually incorporated within its curriculum the teaching that the progressive barber-surgeons of the town had been providing for over two centuries. Its importance as a place of higher education was accepted, but until 1726 it lacked a medical faculty. Leyden University in Holland, which had a long tradition of excellence in medical education and training, sent many of the pioneer medical faculty to Edinburgh in the early eighteenth century. The development of medical education in Edinburgh was further enhanced in 1729, when the Royal Infirmary was opened and attached to the university to provide clinical experience for the students.[29] By the late eighteenth century, Edinburgh had succeeded the continental schools, including Leyden, as the leading medical school in the world. From 1726 to 1799 inclusive, 1,143 men graduated with M.D. degrees from the University of Edinburgh, more than at any other medical school of the eighteenth century.[30]

During that century, when Edinburgh was attaining great success as a university medical complex of the highest caliber, very little was accomplished in London and the provinces of England with regard to university-sponsored medical education. A few private medical schools of questionable quality sprang up in London, and the London Barber-Surgeons began holding lectures and dissections at their guild hall, but interest in both waned as hospital surgeons usurped the clinical teaching function early in the nineteenth century. In June 1827, Warburton presented to the Commons a petition from the Royal College of Surgeons complaining of the regulations of the college. The petition maintained that "the interests of the many were sacrificed for the benefit of the few" and cited a bill that "granted the corporation many powers, among which was the extraordinary one of monopolizing the lecturing on surgery in London; although at that very time many schools of surgery were in existence in the metropolis."[31] The clause was dropped from the 1800 charter, but "the college endeavored by means of bye-laws to obtain a similar authority."[32]

The problem was that the individuals who made up the council of the college were connected with the hospitals and with the lectures delivered at those hospitals. The members of the council of the college therefore had a direct interest in framing the by-laws. "By those bye-laws it was declared, that the only regular schools of Anatomy and Surgery were the hospitals of London, Dublin, Edinburgh, Glasgow and Aberdeen, or . . . a Provincial Hospital containing one hundred patients."[33] Certificates were given to students who studied at one of the aforementioned schools, thereby excluding any other theaters of anatomy and their graduates. By these methods, the hospital surgeons of the Royal College of Surgeons kept control of teaching. During this period the London College of Physicians, although allowing control of teaching to stay with the surgeons, jealously guarded its examining and licensing privileges. The physicians did not become involved with medical education, at the physiological level, remaining content with the medieval tradition of liberal-classical education being carried at Oxford or Cambridge. Most English medical schools, therefore, developed in relation to hospitals and not universities.[34]

Most of the provincial schools in England started as the result of an enthusiast, or a group of enthusiasts, bringing together a number of suitable men prepared to lecture or demonstrate on the various subjects in the medical curriculum, and willing to invest enough money in a common fund to pay for the premises and the expenses of printing. The lecturers provided their own materials for demonstration and shared expenses with other instructors. They usually pooled their fees, which came directly from the students, but gained the majority of their income from private practice.[35]

Teaching at voluntary hospitals began in the eighteenth century and became commonplace in the nineteenth. Voluntary hospitals were often founded by private individuals, many by rich men of the rising middle class. These hospitals were not supported by church, state, or taxpayers, but were maintained by the benefactions of individuals and served by an unpaid medical staff. They were totally philanthropic organizations. The medical staff served the patients as volunteers, but did charge fees to the student physicians who signed on their personal service—much the same arrangement as in the provincial schools.[36] One such voluntary hospital, in 1836, became the Royal Manchester School of Medicine and Hospital; it had begun as a privately funded small infirmary. By the early nineteenth century nearly every county and many provincial towns had such a hospital or infirmary founded and maintained by private benefactors. The urge to be involved in a philanthropic medical project was attested to by Peel, when he spoke to the Commons in 1828: "Many gentlemen have taken up these projects and devoted their time to them from a feeling of pure philanthropy; and I think that a more important subject could not have been chosen."[37]

The Benthamite reformers also were involved in medical education. Education of any kind was dear to their hearts and many had the vision to see that the new science would have to be applied to empirical medicine, if the latter was to progress in the interest of humanity.[38] As early as 1827, ideas of this kind led to the foundation of University College, under the name of the University of London. It was designed to provide inexpensive education for young men who were excluded from Oxford and Cambridge by reason of expense.[39] It was founded with particular emphasis given to the teaching of science and medicine. King's College in London was founded shortly thereafter and had a similar curriculum. Out of these two colleges grew two hospitals with the primary objective of training students, thus finally implementing the Edinburgh example of the university hospital in London.

Much instruction, especially anatomical, in the provincial and London schools depended on a steady supply of cadavers for dissection. Although bodies of executed criminals were often used for this purpose, most schools were chronically short of corpses and resorted to the use of "resurrection men" who rifled graves and purveyed bodies to the teachers. "The exhumators, frequently with a view to raise the price of subjects, to extort money, or to destroy rivalry proceeded to outrageous acts of violence or imprudence, which constantly brought exhumation to light exasperating the public against both the exhumators and the anatomist."[40] Iron fences, still to be found surrounding some graveyards, are a reminder of the heyday of this trade. The Anatomy Act of 1832 empowered the Home Department to issue licenses permitting the lawful acquisition of bodies for the purpose of dissection. This act added some much needed dignity to medical teaching.

Though the Anatomy Act facilitated thorough and comprehensive education of the budding medical profession, the Apothecary Act of 1815 was probably more important. It changed the structure of the three orders, which had remained virtually intact since the Middle Ages. In 1542, by an act initiated by Henry VIII, the apothecaries had won the right to inquire into a patient's symptoms and attempt a diagnosis and prognosis, providing they charged only for the medicine dispensed and not for their advice. In this way, they had become the poor man's doctor. In 1687 the College of Physicians sought to arrest this development by insisting that all of their fellows and licentiates treat the poor free of charge. This insistence, not surprisingly, met with little compliance and consequently, had little effect in controlling the power of the apothecaries. In 1696, the college went further in its attempt to undercut the apothecaries by opening free clinics and dispensing medicine cheaply. This measure proved unproductive also, and in 1703 the physicians decided to take the matter to court to obtain an official ruling. An apothecary named Rose was prosecuted in the lower courts for acting as a physician and lost his case. However, a decision of the House of Lords reversed the verdict, and the right of an apothecary to act as a "general practitioner" was established.[41] The apothecary acting as the poor man's doctor continued, undisturbed, for yet another century.

The 1815 Apothecary Act gave a virtual monopoly to that company to direct the policy as applied to general practitioners. The powers extended to the Society of Apothecaries by the act included control of the guidelines, admittance, and licensing of general practitioners throughout the entire kingdom. The act therefore produced significant changes in the rather chaotic and casual sphere of medical education. It made it compulsory for every student-apothecary and every surgical student who wished to enter "general practice" to attend certain courses of lectures before they could apply to take the necessary licensing examinations. A five-year apprenticeship, prior to the qualifying examination, was also stipulated in the act. The apprenticeship requirement drew special criticism from surgeons and physicians alike. Thomas Wakely, a noted surgeon and physician who edited the medical journal *The Lancet*, suggested that an apprenticeship prior to licensing the general practitioner amounted to "compelling the medical student to pass five of the most valuable years of his life in a state of vassalage and ignorance behind a counter."[42] This was somewhat overstated, for the act stipulated a course of instruction (part of which was devised by the Royal College of

Surgeons itself) alongside the "shop" experience. Wakely also stated that "there is scarcely a clause in the Act which is not manifestly framed with a view of putting money and power into the pockets of these incorporated tradesmen."[43] Wakely spoke for many of the surgical students and members of the Royal College of Surgeons who had hoped to lead the way in the formulation of policy for this new medical professionalism, but had lost out to the apothecaries who had successfully secured the position of leadership through the 1815 act.

The professionalization efforts of the apothecaries quickly encouraged similar developments among the surgeons. In 1800, the old Company of Surgeons became the Royal College of Surgeons. Also, the Napoleonic wars greatly increased the number of surgeons required by the army and navy. Because warfare provides one of the greatest schools of surgery, many surgeons had better practical training than ever before.[44] When peace came, the newly trained surgeons were not content to accept the ill-defined and inferior place previously alloted to them in the medical hierarchy. They demanded equality with the apothecaries in the area of general practice, but the 1815 act excluded them from practice until they met the prelicensing apprenticeship.[45] The College of Surgeons therefore attempted to obtain for itself privileges similar to those granted the apothecaries in the 1815 act, but the legislative attempt failed for the main body of surgeons. The army and navy surgeons did win a victory in 1825 when, via an amendment to the Apothecary's Act, anyone holding a commission in his majesty's service as a surgeon became exempt from the apprenticeship and examination portion of the licensing criteria. The amendment was retroactive to include Napoleonic war veterans.[46] The only course of action left open to nonservice surgeons was to come to private agreement with the Society of Apothecaries to raise the status of its diploma by following the society's rules and regulations. The requirements of these two bodies, the Royal College of Surgeons and the Society of Apothecaries, could be met by an additional course of lectures in surgery and an additional six months spent in the wards of a hospital. It became customary for any ambitious young man to seek qualifications from both "college and hall"—that is, membership of the Royal College of Surgeons and the license of the Society of Apothecaries. So developed the "physician and surgeon," or fully qualified general practitioner.[47]

There were, of course, imperfections in the 1815 act. For example, the act made no provision for examination in midwifery, because childbearing was regarded as a natural function and therefore was not at that time an accepted part of medicine. Also, irregular practitioners continued to enjoy some rights of practice. The druggist, or chemist, was now taking the place of the "old-style" apothecary without benefit of a supervisory body. Not until the passing of the Pharmacy Act of 1852 was there a legal separation between the profession of medicine and pharmacy.[48]

In general, however, the 1815 act proved remarkably successful. Between 1842 and 1844 only 16 licenses were granted by the universities and 37 by the Royal College of Physicians. The remaining English licenses, 953, were granted by "college and hall."[49] The act produced a new group of educated general practitioners in the modern sense, and this new group of practitioners was also radical and energetic. They organized themselves into the reform groups out of which emerged the British Medical Association and the milestone Medical Act of 1858. This act, still the fundamental legal basis of the profession today, was due almost entirely to the demands of medical general practitioners who wished to establish high educational and ethical standards in the profession.

The regulations of the 1815 act and their emphasis on education at once increased the need for more teachers in London and the formation of medical schools in the provinces. During the next few years schools were established in various towns: Birmingham and Sheffield in 1828, Leeds in 1831, Newcastle and Hull in 1832, Bristol and Nottingham in 1833, and Liverpool and York in 1834.[50]

While pressures, stresses, strains, and developments inside the medical community produced a new, stronger focus on improvements in medical education, external factors—primarily the threat and occasional reality of epidemic disease—also contributed fundamentally to the reshaping of health care delivery in England. The nineteenth century had its share of epidemics and threats of nationwide illness that did not develop into real catastrophes but did have an effect on the health-care delivery system and governmental intervention. The first national Board of Health, for example, dates from 1804, when yellow fever threatened to invade Britain. When the threat did not materialize, the board was dissolved, but it set the pattern for future boards and stands as the forerunner of the Ministry of Health and Social Security.

Cholera, an Asiatic disease, did become a reality in Britain in the nineteenth century and profoundly influenced the shaping of the health-care delivery system. Cholera, never endemic in Britain, moved from its point of origin in Central India at the beginning of the nineteenth century; by 1829 it had reached Persia and Siberia, and by 1830 it had invaded Russia and Poland.[51] Its progress, about five miles a day, gave the British authorities time to take action. Cholera reached the Baltic coast in early summer of 1831, and on 21 June, a Central Board of Health was established in England under the supervision of the Privy Council.[52] By 29 June 1831, the board had prepared recommendations and forwarded them to the Privy Council. The report suggested that as there was reason to believe that the disease raging in Russia and northern Europe was in fact infectious, it was necessary that early cases in Britain be detected and publicized. Toward that end, every coastal town or village should establish a local Board of Health to monitor the progress of the disease once it made its appearance in Britain.[53] On 27 October, an army surgeon reported the first British death from cholera in Sunderland. Members of the Central Board of Health traveled about the country encouraging the formation of local boards, instituting isolation hospitals, and advising on treatment. By February 1832 the Central Board employed four deputy inspectors-general of hospitals, twenty-one medical officers and seventeen surgeons. At the end of the epidemic these officers were advising over 1,200 local boards of health, of which 822 were in England and Wales and 400 in Scotland. The epidemic caused about 22,000 deaths before the beginning of June 1832. Then the mortality rate started to decline, and the epidemic virtually ended in December.[54] The Central Board of Health was dissolved in December 1832 when the crisis was over, but the precedent of handling public health emergencies through government intervention and institutions was established. Cholera served as an extremely convincing case study of the usefulness and importance of public health measures.

The 1831–32 cholera epidemic left behind it a concern that slums formed a breeding ground for disease. The government set up a Royal Commission to inquire into the working of the Poor Law, the reason being to find a health care system for the poor. Edwin Chadwick, a lawyer-journalist, was asked to help in the inquiry. In 1833 he presented a report to Parliament that addressed the relationship between preventable "excessive sickness" and poverty.[55] The report was instrumental in promoting a review of the policy for the sick poor in the 1834 Poor Law Reforms. However, the problem was only marginally addressed in the actual Reform Bill; ignoring Chadwick's recommendations for sanitary reform, the New Poor Law gave responsibility for the care of the sick poor to the workhouse.

Cholera returned to Britain in 1848, and again in 1853 and 1867.[56] Although these epidemics never reached the scale of those of bubonic plague, which left so indelible a mark on the pages of history, they did kill tens of thousands. The disease struck swiftly each time, raising local death rates dramatically and stirring even the moribund, unreformed municipal corporations into fits of sanitary activity. But cholera went as quickly as it came and its prevention was relatively simple once its cause in bad water supplies was recognized by John Snow during the second epidemic in 1848.[57] Epidemics were brief, memories short, and municipal purses tight. But if cholera could be ignored, typhus could not.

Typhus, the second most important epidemic disease after cholera, became a major health problem in 1838 when it was carried to England by countless Irishmen flocking to the new industrial cities. It took on the name "industrial typhus" because it found its victims among the industrial laborers, who lived in dirty hovels.[58] Richard Millar, a Glasgow professor of medicine, first drew attention to the connection between poverty and disease in 1833 and observed that typhus "so often attacks the more indigent portion of our operatives during those periodical suspensions of industry that of late years have caused so much distress among that part of our population."[59] Typhus, he concluded, was the "poor man's disease, the product of squalor, insanitation and overcrowding."[60] Whereas cholera had briefly stirred municipal corporations into temporary frantic activity, typhus stimulated concern, investigation, and indignation in the medical profession and reformist circles of a more lasting nature.

Chadwick, who had served on the 1833 Inquiry into the Administration of the Poor Law and the 1834 Poor Law Report, had become secretary of the New Poor Law Commission. He saw the 1838 typhus epidemic as an opportunity for a full-scale investigation into the relationship between poverty and disease. The resultant 1842 Sanitary Report[61] was mainly concerned with the prevention of typhus. This report stimulated creation of the 1844 Metropolitan Health of Towns Association, which empowered a town council to effect sanitary improvements and, more important, to appoint a medical officer of health to oversee the implementation of sanitary reforms as a full-time, salaried official. Liverpool was the first to act, appointing Dr. William Duncan to be the first medical officer of health in Britain in 1846.[62]

Chadwick was well aware that the publication of the Sanitary Report in 1842 was not the end of his work but only the beginning. Rather, the end was public health legislation along the lines suggested in the report's conclusions. The purpose of the report was to influence public opinion, and upon its publication Chadwick set himself the task of vigorously pursuing legislation. Toward this end, he attempted to insure a wide public exposure to the report's findings that disease and poverty were in fact connected by substandard living conditions and poor sanitation.[63] The customary vehicle for propaganda during this period was the *Quarterly Review;* newspapers normally indulged in less discursive comment than their counterparts might today. Chadwick, however, sent copies of the *Sanitary Report* to *The Times* and *The London Morning Chronicle* and both subsequently carried lead articles on the subject.[64] He then succeeded in convincing the *Quarterly Review* to print a long and extremely sympathetic review of the report in the spring of 1843.[65]

The report itself was devoted to establishing four major points. These points were supported by an immense wealth of detail designed to persuade its reader of the urgent necessity for legislative attention to the problem. The first point, comprising more than half the report, established a correlation between poor sanitation, defective drainage, inadequate water supply, and overcrowded housing on the one hand, with disease, high mortality rates, and low life expectancy on the other. The second point was concerned with the economic cost of ill-health, but this was dismissed in a twenty-page chapter. Chadwick's special passion is more discernible in his third point—the social cost of squalor and poverty. His three years of research had impressed upon him the serious damage inflicted by the lack of sanitation on human behavior and morals. His unequivocal statement of this interaction represented a major breakthrough in social thinking. It was a complete reversal of the traditional middle-class attitude that ascribed the miserable circumstances of the poor to defects in their character. Chadwick's fourth point was directed to administration. He found the existing administrative framework too inefficient to deal with matters of public health; he desired a central governmental board to oversee the recommended sanitary reforms. Included in his administrative reform measures was his insistence on the inclusion of properly qualified doctors in the field of public health.

The marked absence of specific recommendations for legislation in the Sanitary Report explains, in part, the long delay in securing parliamentary action. The price of ultimate success was patience and more work. In 1843, Peel's government appointed a royal commission to investigate the health of towns. The commission published two reports the following year. The *First Report of the Health of Towns Commission of 1844* was largely the work of Chadwick. Following the publication of this first report, and in time to influence the recommendations of the commission's final report, Chadwick submitted a complete draft of a parliamentary public health bill to the head of the commission. The final report of the commission did not actually reflect Chadwick's scheme.

Between 1842 and 1845 the main focus of the sanitary reform movement was the Health of Towns Commission, but it was not Chadwick's only line of attack. In addition to official activities, he played an active part in the public opinion campaign. After 1844, agitation was mainly carried on through the medium of the Health of Towns Association. This association, in which a leading part was also played by Lord Ashley, conducted propaganda for sanitary reform through public meetings and publications. Between the founding of the association and the public opinion campaign, Chadwick saw the successful culmination of his efforts in the passing of the Public Health Act in 1848. The act constituted a tentative and uncertain start to government action in the field of health reform, but it was a start.

The new act not only extended the powers of the local authorities, but also gave them greater responsibilities. According to its terms, however, if local authorities proved incapable of carrying out the required improvements, then the centralized General Board of Health was empowered to intervene. However, the general board's administrative status was ill-defined and it proved to have no real power. When, in late 1848, a full-blown cholera epidemic hit Edinburgh, then London, and finally the rest of the kingdom, the general board was given emergency powers. Chadwick then used the act to recruit a special corps of health visitors, increase the number of Poor Law Surgeons, and emphasize the importance and indispensability of Medical Officers of Health upon local authorities. The life of the General Board of Health was originally fixed at five years by the Public Health Act of 1848, but due to yet another cholera epidemic in 1853 it was given a year's extension. The agency was terminated in 1854, after debate in Parliament on its continuance turned into a personal attack on Chadwick and his work. The General Board of Health was a short-lived phenomenon, but its legacy was an increased awareness of public and personal health. Although the demise of the board terminated Chadwick's official career, it did not bring an end either to local activity in the public health field or to central government control; Chadwick's ideas carried on. It has been said that "Chadwick, born in a Lancashire farmhouse where the children were washed all over, every day, seems to have had a desire to wash the people of England all over, every day, by administrative order."[66] Public health work was passed to a newly created committee of the Privy Council where, under John Simon as medical officer, the foundations of the modern public health service were patiently and carefully laid. Yet it was through the Poor Law Commission and then the General Board of Health that the Benthamite formula of inquiry, legislation, execution, inspection, and report was incorporated into the nineteenth-century British health-care delivery system.

This summary suggests that in the nineteenth century there were really two systems of medicine in operation. The first was for those who had the economic means to be independent of government help and could therefore make their own private arrangements with the health professional of their choice. The other involved the Poor Law and took care of the people who, because of economic need, had no choice of doctor. It was in this latter sphere that medical activity escalated in response to need. The 1834 Poor Law Amendment Act required boards of guardians to appoint parish or union doctors. The guardians often drove the hardest bargain possible in recruiting doctors; often the man willing to accept the lowest wages was appointed. A wage of as little as £20 a year was often paid. Out of the sum paid by the guardians, the doctor had to pay for his own medications. This procedure was not conducive to obtaining the most qualified or productive doctors. Agitation for reform of this practice came from the newly qualified general practitioners (college and hall) who favored a single licensing authority and a unified system of qualifiying doctors to practice any branch of medicine in any part of the country. Under the old, unreformed system, the Society of Apothecaries, the universities, and the Royal College of Physicians were all entitled to issue licenses. To confuse the issue further, the graduates of the University of Edinburgh, considered one of the world's best medical schools, were often not allowed to practice in England unless they obtained one of these licenses. The pressures of the great epidemics of mid-century provided stimulus for reform. Another pressure surfaced with the need to appoint Medical Officers of Health within the terms of Chadwick's Act of 1848. It was found that there existed no register of qualified practitioners from which the new officers could be selected. The need for such a register inspired the 1858 Medical Act.

The General Medical Order of 1842, issued by the Poor Law

Commission Office, improved the Poor Law doctor situation somewhat by requiring the local Board of Guardians to hire a qualified doctor at a fixed and equitable rate instead of awarding a contract to the lowest bidding applicant. Now, the parish doctor, usually a private practitioner who wished to augment his income, became a semipublic officer. Due to the 1842 order, the quality of the Poor Law Medical Officer rose. The Medical Order stated that "every Medical Officer should possess both a medical and surgical qualification."[67]

In 1847 Parliament abolished the Poor Law Commission established in 1834 and instituted the Poor Law Board on a year-to-year basis. The rules of the Poor Law Commission with regard to the sick poor were far more humane and adequate than the practice of the local guardians had been. During the ten years following the establishment of the more centralized Poor Law Board, total expenditures on the sick poor increased more rapidly than the number of paupers.[68] This increase was inevitable, because in the middle of the century 72 percent of all pauperism was caused by sickness.[69] The new Poor Law Medical Officer, created by the Medical Order of 1842 and secured by the formation of the Poor Law Board in 1847, was in the forefront of reform for the sick poor.

The Medical Act of 1858, therefore, was the culmination of decades of agitation for medical reform. The avowed reasons for the agitation were that the organization of the medical profession was chaotic, and that the public was misled and exploited by many uneducated quacks and charlatans. The routes of entry were so many and so varied that the public had no way of judging between good and bad medical care. By the time the Medical Act of 1858 was passed, the state was finding itself deeply involved in medical affairs. One could have a laissez-faire economy but it was impossible to have a laissez-faire health policy, as the epidemics had shown. If the state was to employ doctors, then it had to be sure that they were legally qualified.

The 1858 Medical Act placed all the existing licensing corporations under the control of a new and powerful body, the General Council of Medical Education and Registration, henceforth known as the General Medical Council.[70] The council was to be chosen for a term not exceeding five years, and all members of the Council had to be qualified to be registered under the terms of the act. The act gave legal definition to the "qualified medical practitioner," who alone should be eligible for any public appointments or for inclusion in the Medical Register. The General Council was, under the authority of the Privy Council, to supervise the compilation of the Register. The Registrar of the General Council was charged with the annual publication of this alphabetized list of "qualified" individuals along with their address, title, diploma, and degree(s). Only inclusion in this register conferred legal status on the individual. The registrar also was allowed the discretion of removing a name from the register if the "practitioner" was found guilty of a crime or professional misconduct.[71]

The General Medical Council was also empowered to demand information from licensing bodies on their courses of study and examinations, and it abolished the local jurisdictions of the medical corporations. Scottish graduates of medicine were now officially recognized in England and Wales. In 1859 the council appointed its first Committee of Education to evaluate the educational standards of the licensing bodies. The committee reported back with the following recommendations, which were adopted in their entirety: prior to professional study, all students must have passed a General Education examination; only universities could give the examinations; all students had to be registered with a licensing body; no license could be given to anyone less than twenty-one years of age; and four years of professional study was to be required after the General Education examination.[72] The act worked. For the first time in British history, a whole profession submitted itself to a single governing body.

Because the Medical Council assumed the right to suspend inclusion in the register, it was able to formulate an ethical code to which all who were registered had to conform. The ethical code raised the prestige of the doctor and transformed the medical trade into the medical profession. Medical officers of health, Poor Law medical officers, hospital administrators, the fledgling nursing profession, and auxiliary medical personnel all adhered to the ethical code established by the General Medical Council. The picture that emerges from all this is one of revolutionary change. At the beginning of the nineteenth century the medical profession and the health-care delivery system in Britain were divided into various, sometimes conflicting, orders, corporations, hospital systems, and poor relief to the sick. By 1858 the medical profession became a coordinated body of practitioners, under the supervision of a governmental body that protected both the profession and the public by regulating minimum standards of education and admission to the Medical Register. The standards set by centralized government formed the basis for both the public and private health-care delivery systems in mid-nineteenth-century Britain.

Not until this time, however, can one think in terms of a unified medical profession, and even after the 1858 act the profession had not internalized its unity enough to plot and scheme as Thomas Szasz has suggested. His condemnation of "Institutional Psychiatry" and its perpetrators, the "mad-doctors," would imply that the profession was advanced enough as a unified body to become "the conquistadors and colonizers of the mind of man."[73] The evidence, however, indicates nothing of the kind and instead displays a reality of quite the opposite character. Psychiatrists (mad-doctors) are accused of "inventing" or "manufacturing" mental disorders for ignoble reasons, but careful historical investigation of that thesis suggests that other factors account for the development of health care for the mentally ill. As he has repeatedly explained in a long series of publications, but particularly in *The Manufacture of Madness*, psychiatrists inflicted forms of coercion and brainwashing on the oppressed on behalf of the oppressors. Szasz's theory about madness is, therefore, conspiratorial. However, no evidence is presented to support such a theory except that "medicine" replaced "religion" as the tool by which the general populace is kept in line. It can readily be seen that his opinion not factual evidence, supports his theory, and therefore the theory is immune from challenge. The oppressors who benefited from the manufacture of madness appear to be, according to Szasz, society as a whole and physicians in particular. He states, "the aim of the semantic conversion from morals to medicine is embarrassingly clear. *Cui bono?* Who profits from it? The patients? No. The clergyman? No. The physician? Yes."[74]

This study has suggested that even if the profession wanted to indulge in such practices, it was incapable of such a unified effort until well past mid-century. The facts seem to support the arguments of Martin Roth, who attempts to refute Szasz's theory on the basis of lack of evidence. In a recent article,[75] Roth dismisses as absurd Szasz's theory that psychiatrists "invented" mental illness for their own purposes in the eighteenth and nineteenth centuries. He further suggests that "the poets and novelists who anticipated many discoveries of modern psychiatry must have sinned in similar fashion. Szasz would say it is not insight and compassion we find in the words of Macbeth:

Canst thou not minister to a mind diseased,
Pluck from the memory a rooted sorrow,
Raze out the written troubles of the brain,
And with some sweet oblivious antidote

Cleanse the stuff'd bosom of that perilous stuff
Which weighs upon the heart?

but an early verion of the medical model with its depraved phar-
macological practices."[76]

4

THE GROWTH OF SCIENCE AND THE CHANGE IN THE PSYCHOLOGICAL PARADIGM

Knowledge advances by steps, and not by leaps.
—Macaulay, 1831

The asylum system and the health care system came together in the nineteenth century within the social-service delivery system with noticeable results. To understand this phenomenon it is necessary to take note of the change in the psychological paradigm that allowed the two systems to merge and create sweeping institutionalization of the mentally ill in nineteenth-century British society.

The nineteenth century was an era in which the central government advanced into many areas of society previously regarded as either private or local. It was a century of change and consequent conflicts; the industrial revolution brought material wealth and urban poverty, and there was widespread religious revival while the foundations of belief were eroded by equally widespread scientific thought. The latter conflict of epistemology and value structure loomed above all others: the conflict was between the new scientific naturalism and older beliefs in a transcendental spiritual reality. This conflict was resolved in the field of theoretical and applied psychology by a change in the psychological paradigm.

The naturalists, proponents of scientific naturalism, held out the hope of perpetual progress and the perfectibility of man. Defenders of older beliefs clung to traditional concepts of religion and society. In the field of psychology, the epistemology of natural science was optimistic and promised success. It eventually became the orthodox belief and the result was a change in the psychological paradigm dominating the era.

A paradigm, as used in science, is the basic set of assumptions

55

that provides the framework within which scientists work. However, that framework is subject to evolutionary or radical change because science is a collective, public enterprise, and scientists are not free to pursue their own vision of reality. The scientist must submit his ideas to the challenge of public scrutiny through the eyes of his colleagues. Through this process, various concepts compete with one another for acceptance by the scientific community.

In his highly original work *The Structure of Scientific Revolutions*, Thomas S. Kuhn has proposed that a paradigm has two components: the disciplinary matrix and the shared exemplars.[1] The disciplinary matrix consists of a set of usually unstated assumptions. Often these assumptions are unconscious, having been internalized during the learning process and subsequently passed on in the same way. The assumptions are not subjected to empirical testing; however, they form the basis for specific hypotheses, which are then subjected to empirical tests.[2] The other component of a paradigm, the shared exemplars, includes models of research that provide agreed-upon methods used in the investigation of new problems. These methods are held up to the students of science as good examples of patterns to be followed in their own research.[3] An era's particular preeminent psychological paradigm, therefore, will have a disciplinary matrix and one or more shared examplars as part of the paradigm.

According to Kuhn, a change in the currently dominant paradigm will occur in response to a crisis when scientists are confronted with severe and prolonged anomalies in their observations and research.[4] Although Kuhn presents his theory as one of revolutionary changes in scientific thought, the results appear to be more evolutionary in nature. His theory of the process of change is Hegelian in method. Kuhn explains scientific change as analogous to the process of "thesis, antithesis and synthesis" found in Hegel's dialectics.[5] The process, in science, evolves in the following stages: Protoscientists, or Scientists, do not agree on a set of paradigmatic assumptions; infighting and random fact-gathering ensues; one school gains control of the field and ousts its competitors, who are then relegated to pseudoscientific status; an era of agreement on a working scientific paradigm begins, and continues, until. . . ; inevitably a problem is found that resists solution—an anomaly; the anomaly may be explained within the era's existing paradigm, but usually is not; a crisis ensues leading to extraordinary research; the restrictions of the existing paradigm loosen and an alternative paradigm emerges; the alternative paradigm becomes the agreed-upon working scientific paradigm if it succeeds in solving the anomaly (it is this change of the paradigm that Kuhn calls the "revolution"); and the process begins again when an anomaly is encountered.[6]

A psychological paradigm, therefore, consists of all the inflected forms of the disciplinary matrix and shared exemplars existing at any given time in natural science, applied to the mental/emotional condition of humans, as demonstrated by their behavior. A change, or "revolution," in the psychological paradigm can be seen, therefore, as occurring in response to the process outlined by Kuhn. The nineteenth century saw such a change occur in the psychological paradigm, dominant within Western thought, and it profoundly affected the treatment and handling of the mentally ill.

In early and mid-nineteenth-century England, it is the combination of Locke's idea of the perfectibility of man, Bentham's utilitarianism and Comte's biological positivism that governed policies concerning the mentally ill. It is necessary at this point to consider the antecedents of the commonly held psychological views that began the paradigmatic change.

In the midst of the intellectual chaos following the Reformation, philosophers attempted to begin anew; to seek truth unencumbered by the confusion of the past. But the old Platonic/Aristotelian duality persisted. In France, René Descartes founded modern rationalism, basing his source of truth in innate reason. In England, John Locke founded modern empiricism, basing his truth on unbiased observation. They, and others, continued the Scientific Revolution, which, according to Butterfield, reduced the Renaissance and Reformation to mere episodes. To medieval thinkers the world was organized in a divinely ordained hierarchy from God to man to material world. This profoundly spiritual world view was attacked and replaced in the seventeenth century by another view of universal organization that was mathematical and mechanical. Natural scientists demonstrated the mechanical nature of heavenly and earthly phenomena, and finally the mechanical approach was extended to humanity itself. The scientific method of observation, experimentation, and application could be applied to society, if it was ailing, and to man himself if he was not quite fit, physically or mentally. The laws of nature could be sought and found in the material world, society, and the mind of the individual. By the mid-nineteenth century all were considered machines subject to natural law. The shift from the spiritual medieval view to the scientific modern view is apparent through the contemporary thinkers.

Descartes, in the seventeenth century, proposed a speculative psychology based on divinely inspired, innate reason. Putting aside all previous theories, while taking a clue from the Skeptics, he resolved to doubt everything until he found something self-evidently true. Systematically doubting the existence of truth, beginning with God and continuing through the world of man, he realized that by doubting at all he admitted his own self-conscious existence. His first undoubtable truth was expressed as "cogito, ergo sum": I think, therefore I am.

The discovery by reason of self-evident truths, and the deduction from them of other truths is a rationalist method; a deductive method. Although Descartes did not condemn sense perception as Plato did, his deductive method was Platonic. The inductive, or empirical, method stands in contrast to Descartes. He "was not the first to prove his own existence from mental activity; St. Augustine had said, 'if I am deceived, I exist' in the same introspective rationalist tradition."[7] The introspective approach to psychology lasted until the biological approach replaced it in the nineteenth century.

It was not specifically against Descartes, but against the concept of innate, self-evident truths, that Locke reacted. John Locke was a seventeenth-century practicing physician, so it was not unusual that he brought a practical empiricism to his psychological theories. Unlike Descartes, who sought ultimate truth, Locke wished only to know how the mind worked. He rejected the idea that the mind knew forms, essences, or truths, believing that the mind knew only its own ideas formulated from experience. He, of course, attacked the concept of innate ideas, preferring his own concept of *tabula rasa* (blank slate). His psychology was not a simplistic description of mind function, but rather he saw the mind as a "complex information processing device prepared to convert the materials of experience into organized human knowledge."[8]

We can conclude that the differences between Locke the empiricist and Descartes the rationalist were primarily differences of emphasis. Both wanted to transcend sterile scholastic philosophy; both tried to do so by examining the human mind. Descartes was more the captive of the past, still searching with pure reason for eternal truth. Locke pointed more to the empirical future.

The seventeenth century laid the foundation for the Enlighten-

ment of the eighteenth century, when science and reason replaced religion as the chief intellectual institution of society. In
time, Newton's and Locke's empiricism overcame rationalism as
well. Psychology replaced metaphysics as the central philosophical concern of the eighteenth century. By denying innate ideas,
and therefore innate depravity, Locke asserted that people may be
educated and perfected and consequently society enlightened
and perfected. The concept of human perfectibility was a constant
theme during the eighteenth century. This concept had political
repercussions during the eighteenth century and, more important for the subject at hand, a great impact on the treatment of
mental illness during the nineteenth century.

The Enlightenment period began with the empirical world view
as ascendant but not yet prevalent; it ended with its prevalence
over the traditional view of discoverable eternal truth. The Enlightenment was therefore a period of transition between a Platonic world and an Aristotelian world. Philosophers and
protopsychologists alike served as transition figures during the
eighteenth century. By the nineteenth century, the process was
complete although the opposing force made a very impressive
stand in the form of romanticism. Therefore, we see in the nineteenth century, especially obvious in England, empiricism as the
accepted norm being challenged by the declining, traditional
value system. The two-thousand-year-old tension between world
views still existed, but with one very major change—Aristo-
telianism has won general philosophical allegiance.

During the eighteenth century the intellectual torch of British
empiricism passed from Locke to Hume. David Hume, a native of
Edinburgh, extended Locke's theories to include the idea that
knowledge consists of a mere sequence of perceptions, none of
which can be proved to be true. Perceptions are then divided by
Hume into two categories, impressions and ideas. Impressions
were sensations, and ideas were less vivid copies of impressions.
Hume gave priority to impressions over ideas; impressions, received through sense perceptions, had validity, whereas ideas
could be false, corresponding to nothing real (such as the uni-
corn).[9] Truth could be determined by tracing ideas to impressions,
and whatever ideas were found to have no empirical content,
such as the ideas of metaphysics or theology, could be dis-
regarded. Hume also gave priority to simple perceptions over
complex ones, suggesting that complex ideas are built up out of
simple sensations. He thus stated an associationist view of psychological function. Hume formulated three laws whereby per-

ceptions are associated or connected with one another: the principle of resemblance (a picture impels us to think about the original); the principle of contiguity (mention of one room in a building impels us to think about another); and the principle of cause and effect (when we think about a wound, we also think about the subsequent pain).[10] Hume subsequently asserted that the ability to form general conclusions, or habits, is founded on association, on our propensity to generalize from limited instances. He noted that the same tendency to generalize is present in animals, resulting in behavior by habit. This conclusion, based as it was on associationism, is the basis for behaviorist psychology. Fully developed behaviorism is a twentieth-century phenomenon, but a not yet fully articulated theory of behaviorism was present and utilized by nineteenth-century mental health reformers. The idea was: change the habit and the subsequent behavior can be changed.

Another conclusion can be drawn from Hume's assumptions that humans and animals respond to association in a similar way: animals are without "reason," therefore, "reason" must have little to do with animal mental activity, and by extension with human mental activity. Hume's psychology became inextricably intertwined with the doctrine of utilitarianism in the nineteenth century, and helped to put an end to the concept that man, or his world, is rationally ordered.

Hume's ethical theory approached a relativistic morality, based on public opinion. He believed that moral values are based on the opinions of a particular society. Ethical standards that each group condones are called moral, whereas those that the group disapproves are regarded as immoral.[11] As religion declines as the primary institution of society, and once reason is discarded as well, a relative guide to morality is always adopted. Society defines morality according to its own values and standards.

Among the French Enlightenment philosophers, reason had not yet been discarded, although revelation had. Their interests were eclectic and they debated among themselves every topic concerning human knowledge. They were united, however, in their condemnation of the established church and the feudal government that it supported. Although opposing the church, few were atheists; most were deists, believing in a supreme creator, while rejecting the ritual and dogma of organized religion. The main focus of the philosophes' activities was the reconstruction of society according to natural law, inspired by Newton's physics. This orientation is called "naturalism," an understanding of humans in natural rather than supernatural terms.

By the mid-eighteenth century, naturalism was confronted by an ethical crisis. The early philosophes were optimists, their optimism based on the belief that the world was made for humans by a benevolent creator. As the century progressed, however, this optimism seemed unjustified. The great Lisbon earthquake took thousands of lives in a seemingly indiscriminate manner. This occurrence, at least for Voltaire, showed that Newton's machinelike world was indifferent to human life. One solution to the ethical void left when optimism lessened was to make the pleasure/pain principle guide to human behavior more reasonable and prudent, to seek general rather than personal (hedonistic) pleasure. This solution was already implicit in Hume's theories. This was the groundwork of English utilitarianism, which tried to base society on a naturalistic ethic of calculating personal pleasure against societal need. The excesses of the French Revolution pushed philosophy from the grasp of reason (in whose name excesses were committed) into the arms of utilitarianism.

"Utilitarianism was implicit in the teachings of the eighteenth century associationists from Hume onward who said that sensations are either pleasant, which we desire to repeat, or unpleasant, which we desire to avoid. Utilitarianism, simply tried to apply this motivational system to society as a whole."[12] Utilitarianism, an essentially British philosophy of the nineteenth century, defined virtue in terms of utility expressed in the maxim "the greatest good for the greatest numbers." Jeremy Bentham, the doctrine's leading spokesman, defined utility as "that property in any object whereby it tends to produce benefit, advantage, pleasure, good or happiness."[13] These synonymous terms are applicable either to individuals or to the community as a whole. Bentham's major effort, as set forth in *Introduction to the Principles of Moral Legislation* (1789), was to devise a program of good government based solely on the principle of utility, disregarding any considerations of historical context or human rights. In the first half of the nineteenth century, England showed a decided tendency toward utilitarian legislation. By mid-century, treatment and legislation regarding the mentally ill showed the effect of utilitarian doctrine combined with the biological view of the individual as suggested by positivism.

As natural science and technology marked success after success, a general attitude called "scientism" spread a faith in the ability of science to answer all questions and solve all problems. Auguste Comte, in early nineteenth-century France, named this general attitude positivism. As an epistemology, positivism, guided by Comte, adopted a radical empiricism. Human knowledge would be confined to the collection and correlation of facts that would yield an accurate description of the world. With this knowledge an ability to predict the natural world would commence. Subsequently, with the ability to predict nature would come the ability to control nature.

> Comte believed that it would be possible to list the individual sciences in order of their complexity, from the simplest to the most complex, that the complex sciences would be seen to depend upon simpler ones, and that the more complex sciences would appear later than the simpler ones related to them. He constructed a hierarchy of the sciences on this basis as follows: Mathematics, Astronomy, Physics, Chemistry, Biology—which includes Psychology, and Sociology.[14]

Comte disapproved of introspective psychology, which he regarded as metaphysical. He held out some hope for phrenology, which tried to tie personality traits to distinct areas of the brain. He divided psychology in two: the study of the individual he assigned to physiology and biology; the study of humans as social animals he assigned to sociology.[15]

In 1974 William F. Bynum outlined the three major views of the causes of mental illness found in the British psychiatric literature of the late eighteenth and early nineteenth centuries: that insanity is always attended by structural changes and thus is ultimately a physical condition; that insanity is always a mental condition, properly differentiated from the physical disease that secondarily produces mental symptoms; and that insanity may be caused by either physical disease or mental aberrations.[16] The majority of British physicians who expressed themselves on the subject of insanity during this period subscribed to the first position—that insanity was a physiological process, a disease of the body.[17]

Until the early modern period, psychology was essentially a part of philosophy. By the late eighteenth century, however, we see psychology being viewed as part of science. The view of man as a biological animal assumed, or suggested, a potential for cure. Until this time treatment of the mentally ill was based on keeping the individual from harming himself or others, while all waited for God to heal him or for his innate reason to surface.

> One of the most notable features of the pre-nineteenth-century literature on madness is its almost exclusive emphasis on disturbances of the "reason," or the higher intellectual faculties of man. Insanity was conceived as a derangement of those faculties which were widely assumed to be unique to man; as a matter of fact, we sometimes find

in the literature the presumed absence in animals of any condition analogous to insanity taken as proof that man's highest psychological function results from some principle totally lacking in other animals, that is, the soul.[18]

It was this world view that nineteenth-century mental health reformers and physicians modified in favor of biological psychology. This was primarily the achievement of Franz Joseph Gall, the founder of what became popularly known as phrenology. In 1800 Gall published *On the Human Brain*, in which he concluded that philosophic concepts were useless for the specific empirical investigations that science requires.

> There is abundant evidence to substantiate the claim that phrenology completely reoriented psychiatric thought. Briefly, this reorientation can be seen as the shift in psychiatry to an interpretation of mental illness as related to scientific community once and for all that the brain (not the soul) is the organ of the mind, and argued strongly that both its structure and functions could be concomitantly analysed by observation rather than speculation.[19]

The principle tenet of phrenology was that psychological traits and aptitudes were located in distinct areas of the brain, and could be assessed by an inspection of the skull. The old philosophical use of the term *faculty of the mind* was transformed both medically and popularly into the notion of faculties as the functions of specific cerebral parts and often made to be synonymous with the parts themselves.[20] The use of the concept *faculty* is found in Western philosophy as early as Aristotle and a medieval schematic of faculties was worked out by Ibn-Sina (Avicenna), but with Gall we have the first modern faculty scheme based on empirical (although faulty) research. K. M. Dallenbach concluded that "phrenology is the matrix from which our term 'faculty' is derived," and that only after Gall and his student Spurzheim had propagated the doctrine did "mental functions" take on its present meaning.[21]

Gall correlated specific behavior functions (faculties) with the particular region of the brain responsible for the function (corresponding faculty). Although he carried out detailed anatomical studies of the brain and nervous system, he found the techniques of his time too crude to answer the questions he posed, so he turned to a unique methodology.

> Gall assumed that well-developed faculties would correspond to well-developed parts of the brain. Those "organs" corresponding to the

well-developed faculties in the brain would be larger than those organs corresponding to less developed faculties, and their relative size would be registered on the skull as bumps overlying the developed organ. Empirically, then, Gall's method was to show that people possessing certain striking traits would possess skulls with bumps over the corresponding organs of the brain, and that weak traits would go with undeveloped brain-organs and skull-regions.[22]

Gall's principle disciple, Spurzheim, settled in London in 1814 and was instrumental in the introduction of phrenology to England. He lectured extensively throughout the country until his death in 1832. By that time, the doctrine had gained a significant hold on scientific and medical opinion. In 1832 there were no less than twenty-nine phrenological societies in Great Britain.[23] The British Phrenological Association was founded in 1835, and counted among its members ten superintendents of public asylums as well as many distinguished psychiatrists of the period.[24] By 1833 the subject of phrenology had gained sufficient standing among medical professionals to be lectured on at the London Hospital, St. Thomas' Hospital, Grainger's Theater of Anatomy, Dermott's School of Medicine, and the University of London. In medical schools outside London it enjoyed similar success; courses in the subject were established in Manchester, Glasgow, and Edinburgh.[25] E. H. Ackerknecht concluded that "Gall's doctrine was at least as influential in the first half of the nineteenth century as psychoanalysis was in the first half of the twentieth."[26]

Phrenology, of course, was eventually found to be inaccurate and was rejected as a pseudoscience, but not before it had led to the establishment of a physiological psychology pioneered by W. B. Carpenter. A physician, Carpenter became the leader of the new school of physiological psychology. He was installed as Fullerian Professor of Physiology at the Royal Institute in 1835 and made a Fellow in the Royal Medical Society. He continued his scientific research and in 1835 published General and Comparative Physiology; in 1842 he published Principles of Human Physiology. The latter work was expanded and published in 1874 as Principles of Mental Physiology; it contained the definitive statement of Carpenter's psychological views. It was his advocacy of the doctrine of unconscious cerebral functioning that led to the theory's general acceptance.

Carpenter's school was in no sense a formal organization, but his followers included many eminent medical and scientific figures of the day who realized the importance of physiological psychology. The senior member of the group was Sir Benjamin Brodie, court surgeon to George IV and William IV and professor of comparative anatomy and physiology at the Royal College of Surgeons as well as the first president of the General Medical Council.[27] Another follower of Carpenter was Henry Holland, a most sought after physician in Victorian London, who numbered among his patients six prime ministers and was personal physician to Queen Victoria. Holland wrote a series of papers that were published as a collection in 1853 titled *Chapters of Mental Physiology*. The most learned member of the group was T. Laycock who taught at the renowned University of Edinburgh. He published a comprehensive, systematic treatise on brain interactions in 1859 titled *Mind and Brain*. As the preceding sketches suggest, this group was no motley collection of crackpots, as the phrenologists have come to be seen; it was the cream of the medical crop.

By midcentury, phrenology's scheme of brain location had been firmly rejected. Carpenter himself sounded the death knell of the doctrine in a review of a phrenological text in 1846. He replaced the spurious localization ideas of the phrenologists with a broad theory of levels of motor function and reflex action that retains validity even today.[28] Gall's theory had opened two directions of inquiry, one scientific and one occult. Scientifically, it was the inspiration for men like Carpenter to pursue research into the localization of brain function. For that reason the doctrine can be viewed as a turning point in psychology. Once phrenology had lost its scientific credibility, however, the occult direction was picked up by a portion of the lay society and was taken to an extreme. The foolishness of its dying years is unfortunately the way it is remembered, rather than for the groundwork it laid for further research that led to fundamental changes in psychological thought.

Reviewing the criteria Kuhn lays down for describing a change in a paradigm and integrating the actual change in the Psychological Paradigm, it can be seen that, according to Kuhn, the following pattern emerged:

1. A period of normal science must precede the change. In this case the period of normal science that preceded the change was in the form of philosophical psychology.
2. In the course of conceptualization one or more serious anomalies are discovered. In this case the anomaly occurred between rationalism and empiricism.

3. The anomaly must resist solution, precipitate a crisis and a loosening of paradigmatic restrictions. In this case the anomaly resisted solution and precipitated a crisis within natural science (naturalism).

4. At some point a rival paradigm must emerge, one that can explain the anomalies. In this case a rival paradigm emerged in the form of biological (rather than philosophical) psychology.

5. As the crisis deepens, the new paradigm attracts adherents of scientific respectability. In this case the new biological paradigm attracted adherents of scientific respectability—first with phrenology and then with physiological psychology.

6. After a period of struggle the field is redefined according to the new paradigm and a new kind of normal science is pursued. In this case the new paradigm, physiological psychology, was, and still is, accepted as normal science.

7. The change agent is relegated to a position of pseudoscience. In this case phrenology was relegated to the position of pseudoscience.[29]

Therefore, although the development of psychology appears to be evolutionary, and to some extent is, Kuhn's criteria for the change of a paradigm is met at the end of the eighteenth and the beginning of the nineteenth century. By the mid-nineteenth century the dominant paradigm was no longer philosophical but physiological.

Within the framework of this new psychological paradigm existed the potential for the cure of mental illness. This cure potential motivated both physicians and reformers to revamp the asylum system. In the field of mental illness, the nineteenth century became an era of optimism; implied cure promised success in turning mental illness into mental health. Although the intent was well founded and well intentioned, the technology was absent, dooming the reformers to failure. The Victorian reformers, lacking the twentieth-century hindsight of their critics, proceeded, in good faith, within their era's dominant paradigm.

5

THE MYTH OF MORAL MANAGEMENT
AND THE GREAT UNWANTED

What is all knowledge but recorded experience—a product of
history.

—Thomas Carlyle, 1858

The theory of social control of the lower classes of society by a
medical profession representative of the dominant middle class
appears to be based on the theorists' interpretation of "moral
treatment" and "moral causes" of insanity. The social control theorists have lumped these two concepts together, terming the
aggregate *moral management*. In the words of Andrew Scull,
"Moral treatment actively sought to transform the lunatic, to re-
model him into something approximating the bourgeois ideal."[1]
Moral managers, it is argued, replaced physical coercion with
moral coercion, bluntly, to brainwash the patients in their care.

These conclusions may be the result of semantic misinterpreta-
tion with regard to the word *moral*. To today's reader (and perhaps
researcher) the word moral when encountered in the nineteenth-
century asylum literature carries a different connotation than that
which the original authors intended. "Moral treatment," to the
modern reader, often suggests treatment by indoctrination to
produce correct moral behavior. Similarly, the phrase "moral
causes of insanity" means to us that the patient had erred in his
morality, causing his own insanity. Moral management would
then subsequently imply that correct management of the patient's
moral sensibilities would help him overcome his illness. There is
evidence to suggest that these semantic connotations are not valid
for the nineteenth century.

Moral treatment in the nineteenth century generally meant
mildly humane treatment, in contrast to previous inhumane treatment of the insane. Moral cause, at that time, meant psychological
or psychosomatic rather than physical cause. Moral management
meant, therefore, asylum treatment and recognition of the dif-

ference between (psychological) moral and (biological) physical causes of mental illness. The social control theorists, often sociologists, appear not to appreciate the differences between the nineteenth- and twentieth-century use of these terms. The nineteenth-century terminology reflects the practical application of the new biological paradigm, the development of which we have previously traced.

As Michel Foucault, in *Madness and Civilization*, has repeatedly pointed out, the eighteenth century saw insanity as the absence of reason; the purpose of treatment was to return reason to the patient. "Purification of the body" to allow for the return of reason and the "awakening of the body" to returned reason were behind most treatment schemes. Purification and awakening often took on rigorous and overtly cruel and inhumane forms of treatment, all purportedly aimed at allowing the patient's natural state of reasonableness to resume. Foucault cites Purification treatment as burning and cauterizing to produce the effect of relieving the body of infection through the newly made open wounds.[2] Foucault also cites "immersion" as another form of purification treatment. "Here we find the theme of ablution, with all that relates it to purity and rebirth."[3] An eighteenth-century example of immersion was the surprise bath. Patients would be surprised by being pushed over backward into a pool of water. "Such violence promised the rebirth of a baptism."[4]

John Conolly, resident physician at Middlesex Asylum, describes this earlier practice with horror:

> In some continental asylums the patients were chained in a well and the water gradually allowed to ascend, in order to terrify the patient with the prospect of inevitable death. Another cruel device allowed an unsuspecting patient to walk across a treacherous floor; it gave way, and the patient fell into a bath of surprise, and was there half drowned and half frightened to death.[5]

In addition to purification of the body, treatments were devised to "awaken" the body to reason. One method of "awakening" was used in 1777 on patients with convulsions in the city hospital in Haarlem. When an epidemic of convulsions occurred and antispasmodics did not alleviate the symptoms, Dr. Boerhaave, the medical director, had stoves filled with burning coals ready to heat red hot irons, which, he announced, were ready to burn to the bone the arm of any convulsive who refused to return to a reasonable state on his own initiative.[6] Suggestions were even made to send patients into caverns infested with harmless snakes to awaken them to reason; fortunately, this particular form of shock treatment was never used.[7] Chains and whips, however, were not uncommon methods of physical control, awakening, and purification. However, once the paradigm had changed, these methods became as outmoded as the world view they represented.

The change that occurred at the turn of the century coincided with the emergence of therapeutic optimism and faith in the possibility of cure. That new optimism and faith were inspired by the biological view of mental illness and a confidence in science to find an answer to this confounding ailment. With the reassessment of the nature of insanity came the adoption of new methods of treatment. Pinel's dramatic gesture of striking the chains from the patients at Salpêtrière and Bicêtre asylums in Paris, although legendary, was not just the action of one unique individual. It represented the view, shared by many, that humane treatment was justified within the new psychological paradigm. Pinel, himself, stated the new view succinctly:

> To repeat the maxims which were delivered by the Ancients upon the art of treating maniacs with kindness, firmness and address, can throw light upon the moral management of insanity. Those precepts are only of partial utility [however] as long as the physiology of the disease is not established upon clear and extensive views of its causes, symptoms and varieties.[8]

Esquirol also, in his *Treatise on Insanity*, echoed the sentiments of the early nineteenth-century reformers:

> It is, doubtless, less difficult to establish systems, and to imagine brilliant hypotheses respecting mental alienation, than to observe the insane, and put up with the disgusting circumstances of whatever kind, to which those are exposed, who would, by observation, study the history of this most serious infirmity. Thus, in a general view of the treatment of the insane, we should propose the skillful control of the mind and passions. We must never lose sight of the physical causes which have predisposed to, and provoked insanity; nor by any means ignore the habits of the patient, and the sickness which existed, previous to the appearance of mental alienation.[9]

The nineteenth-century prescription for the treatment of the insane embodied basic humanitarian values that represented a revulsion against earlier inhumane attitudes. When the disturbed individual came to be seen as a biological creature with a biological illness, there remained no purpose in trying to change him from an unreasonable to a reasonable being through torture and fear. When the diagnosis for admission to an asylum was made, a cause for the ailment was also listed. Causes varied widely and included grief, abuse, change of residence, intemperance of drink, sensual excess, and general paralysis (syphilis). These causes were categorized as either moral or physical and bear little resemblance to the categorization employed today. For example, "intemperance of drink" and "sensual excess" were listed as physical causes and "receiving of abuse" was listed as a moral cause. These examples, and others, lend credibility to the idea that many researchers have misunderstood the semantic use of the term *moral cause*. Moral mangement, therefore, became a coalescence of humane asylum treatment and a distinction between the psychological (moral) and biological (physical) causes for the purpose of correct treatment plans and possible cure.

The new humane treatment was first implemented by William Tuke in 1792 at the Retreat at York. Tuke was a Quaker and the retreat was originally a facility primarily for relatives of Quakers. A great-grandson of the founder, Daniel Hack Tuke, a visiting medical officer to York, wrote *Reform in the Treatment of the Insane* in 1892. In that work he outlines the primary objectives in the founding of the retreat.

> First, the revulsion from the inhumanity which had come to light rendered it necessary that the fundamental principles of moral treatment should be those of kindness and consideration for the patients. They were the basis of the proceedings which were taken; in fact, as we have seen, they were carved upon the very foundation stone of the building.[10]

A second objective was to provide an atmosphere congenial to the habits and principles of those for whom the institution was intended—Quakers.[11] Third, says Tuke, acres were to be set aside for cows and gardens for the patients' recreational use, and employment was to be offered as well.[12]

The therapeutic value of physical work and exercise and their inclusion into humane treatment had been suggested on many occasions. Rev. William Mosely, who wrote *Eleven Chapters on Nervous and Mental Complaints* in 1838, commented "that disease in the organ of the brain, and not in the mind, is the cause of nervous complaints and insanity."[13] He therefore concluded that "absence of appropriate exercise and occupation is a predisposing cause of illness."[14] He also noted that the brain had to be used to improve—to leave it idle led to deterioration and incompetency.

> The physiological explanation of this fact is simple and interesting. Arterial or oxyginated blood is the essential element of nutriment to every organ. It is the means of repairing their lost power, and of stimulating their vital energies. The chief local effect of exercise is to increase the action of the blood-vessels, and the nerves and to cause a more rapid and plentiful supply of blood and of nervous energy and thereby to increase the vigour of every part.[15]

Moral management, as least as defined by Rev. Mosely, was clearly based on the newly emergent physiological psychological paradigm just surveyed.

Having implemented this humane treatment program at York with considerable success—Tuke claimed a 90 percent cure rate—his ideas were adopted to some degree in many other asylums, both public and private. The pattern for the replacement of inhumane treatment is described by Robert Gardiner Hill, resident medical officer at Lincoln Asylum, when he outlined the plan in his 1839 work *Total Abolition of Personal Restraint in the Treatment of the Insane:*

> But, it may be asked, what mode of treatment do you adopt in place of restraint? How do you guard against accidents? How do you provide for the safety of the attendants? In short, what is the substitute for coercion? The answer may be summed up in a few words: Classification—watchfulness—vigilant and unceasing attendance by day and by night—kindness—occupation—and attention to health, cleanliness and comfort. This treatment, in a properly constructed and suitable building, with a sufficient number of attendants always at their post, is best calculated to restore the patient; and all instruments of coercion and torture are rendered absolutely and in every case unnecessary.[16]

During the initial period of moral (humane) management, the new diagnosis of moral insanity was made. The term moral insanity was first used by James Cowles Prichard, the Bristol ethnologist and physician, who defined the term as follows:

> This form of mental disease consists of a morbid perversion of the feelings, affections, habits, without any hallucination or erroneous conviction impressed upon the understanding; it sometimes coexists with an apparently unimpaired state of the intellectual faculties.[17]

Madness is located in inappropriate emotions and feelings rather than in defective reasoning.

This diagnostic terminology is often confused by modern researchers with causation terminology. *Moral insanity* was a diagnosis—the actual name of an affliction. *Moral cause* refers to the cause, not to the illness itself, of an affliction. Although moral insanity might very well have the connotation of some defect in the patient's morality, moral cause does not. Again we see probable confusion on the part of some modern researchers as to the correct understanding of nineteenth-century word usage.

Dr. John Conolly provides a vivid description of the reception received by a patient into an asylum practicing moral management.

> The wretched clothes are removed; the patient is taken gently to the bath-room, and has, probably for the first time, the comfort of a warm-bath; which often occasions expressions of remarkable satisfaction. The refreshed patient is taken out of the bath, carefully dried, and has clean and comfortable clothing put on. He is then led to the day-room, and offered good and well prepared food. The very plates, and knife and fork, and all the simple furniture of the table are clean. A patient seen after these preliminary parts of treatment is scarcely to be recognised as the same patient who was admitted only an hour before. The non-restraint treatment has commenced; and some of its effects already appear.[18]

One finds it difficult to doubt the sincerity of such a description.

Public as well as private asylums adopted the methods of moral treatment to some extent; the observation of moral causes and the consequent moral management was widely practiced by midcentury. Although it cannot be denied that some "moral brainwashing" did creep into the system, it appears not to have been based on that objective. The potential for cure within a humane treatment system appears to be the primary objective of the moral managers. The words of a contemporary, Dr. John Conolly, say it well: "But it is a part of the non-restraint system to remember, whatever the state and circumstances of the newly admitted patient may be, that he comes to the asylum to be cured, or, if incurable, to be protected and taken care of."[19]

The decades immediately following the parliamentary investigations represent for British psychiatry a period of therapeutic optimism. Both lay reformers and medical practitioners were anxious that insanity be recognized as a disease and that the insane be placed in hospitals and asylums rather than jails and workhouses. They were also prepared to adopt many of the aspects of moral management, although they "were not prepared to jettison their medical models of insanity; nor were they willing to compromise their central roles in the diagnosis and treatment of the mentally ill. They were successful in establishing the medical speciality of psychiatry."[20]

The social control theorists, especially Szasz and Scull, interpret the reform movement as the result of a desire on the part of asylum doctors to create a specialty for themselves, and consequently neglect the reformers' professed goals of humanitarianism and benevolence.[21] This is an oversimplified view that ignores not only the professed goals of the reformers, but the probability of diversity among the reformers themselves.

The concept of social control has leaped abruptly to prominence—Scull is now widely quoted as an authority on nineteenth-century mental illness—and has been eagerly adopted by historians of the phenomenon who are anxious to escape from the "poverty of empiricism."[22] This desire to escape empiricism has led, unfortunately, to unsubstantiated statements such as, "Very early on in the history of the asylum, it became apparent that its primary value to the community was as a handy dumping place to which to consign the awkward and unwanted, the useless and potentially troublesome."[23] This judgment by Scull is reiterated frequently: "I have suggested that asylums were largely dumps for the awkward and inconvenient of all descriptions." And "From the moment most asylums opened, they functioned as museums for the collection of the unwanted."[24] The social control concept advanced by Scull—that the "great unwanted," a group defined as those not useful in the market economy of mature capitalism, made up the mid-nineteenth century asylum population—is stunningly refuted by statistical evidence.

Andrew Scull's methodology used to reach these conclusions is questionable. Of nine charts used as statistical evidence in his study, six were compilations made by the Commissioners in Lunacy for various years from 1844 to 1891, and three were compilations derived from secondary sources; all were aggregate statistics. The only "proof" these numbers offer is that the majority of lunatics in asylums after 1845 were paupers. From this "fact" he extrapolates that all of these people were "the great unwanted." No statistical evidence is offered to support that assertion. The statistical evidence in the present study was collected to check the validity of Scull's assertions. This study relies on primary source statistics, not already aggregated sources, the assumption being that personally collected and verified evidence is superior in quality and that more than one dimensional (pauper) evidence is required to make valid statements.

The study sample of 2,004 case histories was gathered from the admission records obtained at Haydock Lodge, Bethlehem Hospital, and Essex County Asylum for the years 1845 to 1862.[25] The information given in each of these case histories included: age, sex, marital status, number of children, occupation (from which was derived social status), education, literacy, diagnosed disorder, etiology (cause) of disorder, medications prescribed, and by whose authority the patient was committed. These variables were coded, assigned values, and computerized for the purpose of comparison and further statistical evaluation. At this point, a review of the methodology used in this study is necessary so that the study can be replicated according to the rules implicit in the "scientific method" of statistical research.

A packaged program, Statistical Package for the Social Sciences (SPSS), was chosen to aggregate and manipulate the data. This program allowed for the collation of data on the subjects chosen for this study. The frequency distribution subprogram computes and presents one-way frequency tables and a number of descriptive statistics.[26] In this study, the absolute frequency of each subject was displayed. The descriptive statistics chosen indicated male/female breakdown; married/single comparison; age, including minimum, maximum, mean, and median; average number of children, including mean and median age; an occupational breakdown into six social class groups; categorization and frequency of disorder; medications dispensed; categorization and frequency of the disorder's cause; frequency of nine categories of authority by which patient was committed; average years of education of patient; literacy frequency; private/pauper breakdown; and mortality data.

Another subprogram option utilized displayed cross-tabulations of specific data sets. A cross-tabulation—"a joint frequency distribution of cases as defined by the categories of two or more variables."[27]—is a commonly used method for displaying and subsequently analyzing data used in the social sciences.

The study sample consisted of 2,004 case histories; 983 males and 1,021 females. This random sample corresponds favorably to the population as a whole, as figure 1 shows.[28]

Figure 1 uses the percentages of institutionalized males and females as they relate to the total population. The adjusted population is the result of deleting those persons aged zero to fourteen

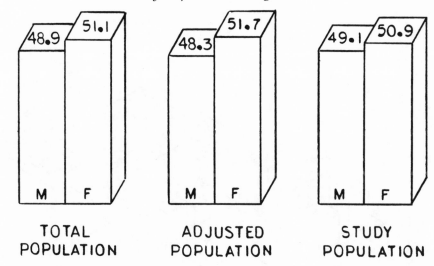

Fig. 1. Male/Female Population Comparison

from the census figures to achieve an accurate comparison, because the study population does not contain anyone under the
age of fifteen. The census figures for 1851, as presented in *European Historical Statistics*,[29] were used as the basis for the population
figures presented, as they are regarded as reliable and fall midway
in our time frame. The census of 1851 shows a total population of
17,927,600 with 8,781,200 males and 9,146,400 females. Adjusting
to delete both males and females under fifteen years leaves a total
population of 11,573,800 with 5,590,100 males and 5,983,700
females. This adjustment reduces the total population by 35 percent but, as can be seen, does not significantly alter the proportions of males to females. Males and females are more or less
equally represented within the institutions surveyed and their
numbers parallel the general population.[30]

In an effort to further support the male/female proportions of
the study population as they relate to actual adjusted population,
Figure 2 was constructed using the data as described previously.

Variance occurs at ages forty to fifty-nine; these variances are
3.8 and 4.2 percent respectively. A number of studies have analyzed the question of whether a particular age group is most
vulnerable to mental illness. Reviewing twenty-four such studies,
Bruce and Barbara Dohrenwend[31] reported that in five the maximum rate appeared in adolescence; in twelve of the studies the
largest numbers were found to be in their middle years; and in
seven studies, the elderly were overrepresented. These studies

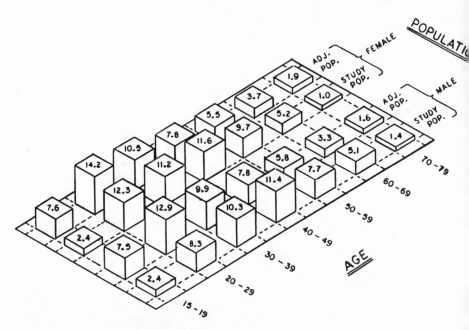

Fig. 2. Sex/Age Population Comparison

represented research both historical and contemporary and, although not conclusive, the fact that twelve of the twenty-four (50 percent) studies reviewed showed higher patient numbers during the middle years of life suggests that the present study is comparable to previous ones with regard to age distribution.

Using the same statistical sources, a comparison of the married, single, and widowed status of the general population to the study population was undertaken (Figure 3). The population unadjusted for the 35 percent of the total under fifteen years of age shows a marked difference from the adjusted population in all but the widowed category. Comparing adjusted population, that is males and females over the age of fourteen, to the study population, no significant difference occurs. The greatest difference is 5.1 percent between the single females in the study population and the single females in the adjusted general population. This does not represent a serious basis on which to present any conclusions. However, it is interesting to note that many of the institutionalized single females were employed as domestics. Another point of interest is that the widowed population is more representative of the general population. Although not statistically significant in

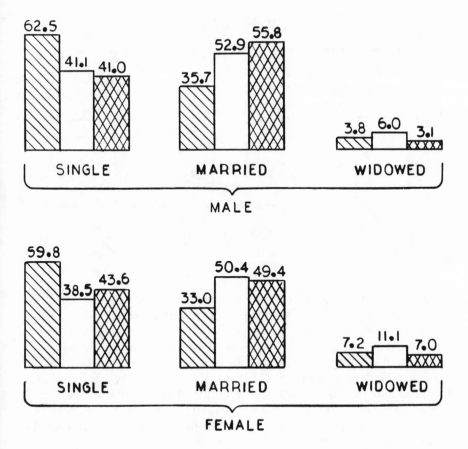

Fig. 3. Marital Status/Sex Population Comparison

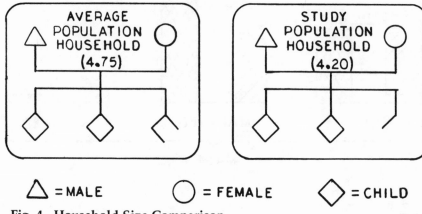

△ = MALE   ○ = FEMALE   ◇ = CHILD

Fig. 4. Household Size Comparison

numbers, the observation could be made that widowed males and females alike were coping with the situation of widowhood, either alone or with the help of others, outside the institution.

The number of children reported for the inmates in the study population range from 0 to 14. Of the inmates, 9.8 percent reported having 3 children, 8.7 percent reported having 7 children. The mean (average number of children reported) was 2.2 children. This does not suggest an "unusual number of children" as a variable with which to cast the inmate into the category of the "unusual" or "unwanted" in society.[32]

Figure 4 presents an ideographic notation for domestic groups[33] comparing the accepted standard for "English household size between the seventeenth and twentieth centuries"[34] (and therefore valid for the nineteenth century) and the ideographic notation constructed according to the statistical portrait already drawn for the asylum study population. Again, the similarity is apparent.

The economic status of the study population (Figure 5) was reported at 68 percent pauper and 32 percent private patients. Of the number of pauper patients, females represented 47 percent and of the private patients females represented 63 percent. Prior to any generalizations with regard to the economic status of the study population, it should be noted that institutions were built (in the case of county asylums) to care for those who could not care for themselves financially. To gain entrance to these facilities it was necessary to declare pauper status. A lunatic was termed a pauper if the money for his maintenance came in whole or in part from public funds.

If we look beyond the simple private/pauper status and analyze the stated (upon admission) occupations of those persons in the study, the evidence presented in Figure 6 shows that the majority of those persons were considered by the admitting authority[35] to possess an occupation. Forty-four percent were considered employable (at least until their illness) in the labor and service sector and 25 percent were considered employable in the trades, artisan, and clerical sector.[36] Criminals and dregs (vagrants) made up only 11 percent of the total.

Males made up 43 percent of the labor and service occupations, 54 percent of the trades and clerical, 85 percent of the criminal segment, and 60 percent of the dregs (Figure 7).

Table 1 was constructed from the stated occupations of the study population after deleting those who did not state an occupation (16 percent) and the criminal element (8 percent). The social class breakdown used in this study includes wealth—to suggest inherited wealth or title; professional—to suggest generally recognized professions involving advanced education and community prestige; trades—to suggest the artisan and clerical category including skilled workers; labor—to suggest unskilled or semiskilled workmen; and dregs—to suggest vagrants. This classification was selected because the five-class breakdown is the

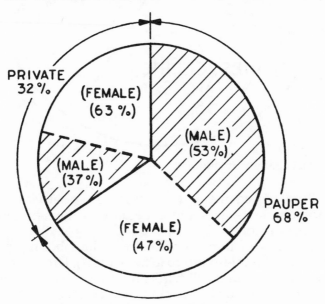

Fig. 5. Status Breakdown by Sex

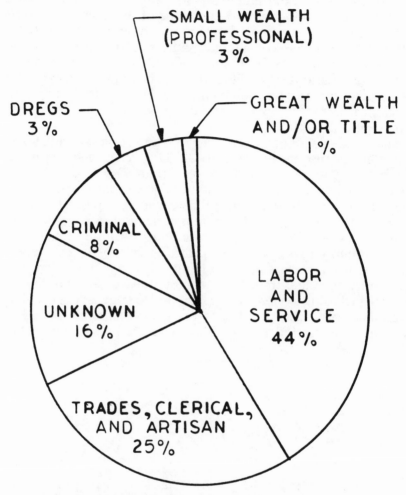

Fig. 6. Occupation Breakdown

generally accepted method of assessing social class.[37] A sixth category, criminals, was added because of their presence in the asylum population.

The majority of inmates were from the laboring group (58.7 percent) and the trades group (32.7 percent). Dregs (vagrants and what we today would call hardcore unemployed) made up only 4.3 percent of the total. It could be stated that this 4.3 percent is Scull's "great unwanted," and, if so, it obviously is not statistically significant and will therefore be discounted. Utilizing the factual

data available, it can be seen that those persons declaring themselves paupers in order to receive treatment nevertheless were
considered as possessing an occupation. Of the declared paupers,
68.7 percent were considered as being part of the laboring class
and 24.1 percent as part of the trades category. Parallels can be
drawn between the "paupers" in the study and welfare recipients
of today. In today's society, if a person requires extensive health or
mental health care, he or she may register for Medicaid as-
sistance. In this process a person must declare that his financial
situation is such that he cannot afford treatment and be certified as
a welfare recipient or, in nineteenth-century language, a pauper.

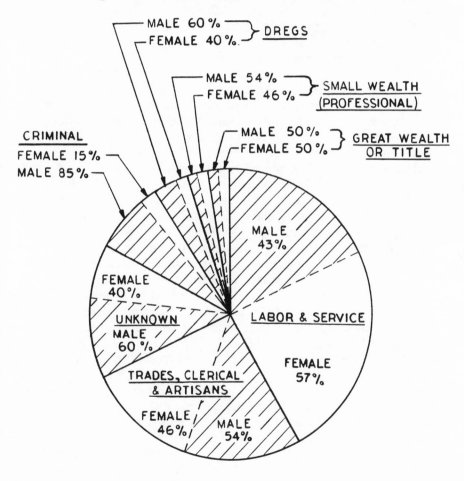

Fig. 7. **Occupation Breakdown by Sex**

Table 1
Social Class/Asylum Status

Social Class	Total (%)	Private (%)	Declared Pauper (%)
Wealth	0.1	0.2	0.1
Professional	4.2	11.0	0.7
Trades	32.7	49.7	24.1
Labor	58.7	39.1	68.7
Dregs	4.3	0.0	6.4

Another parallel can be drawn to today's medical (in particular, mental health) situation. Often the most elaborate and newest facilities are designated for private-pay and Medicaid recipients alike; similarly, in our period of study the newest and best-equipped facilities were the county asylums. There is no way to determine how many paupers declared themselves paupers to receive treatment, or how many were actually paupers. What can be said is that most of the inmate population was considered as possessing an occupation, as did the admitting agents of the asylums. Again, the statistical evidence does not suggest that they were viewed as unwanted and useless to society.

The aggregated case histories of patients residing in Bethlehem Hospital in 1848 shows the literacy and education rate (as reported by the inmates themselves) and suggests that a total of 82 percent of the inmates claimed to be literate or well educated (Figure 8). This result could reflect personal bias or boasting, but again, it does not suggest the type of inmate population that would be considered useless and unwanted by society.

In summary and in answer to the statement that "from the moment asylums opened, they functioned as museums for the collection of the great unwanted," the evidence presented shows that the inmate asylum population in this study corresponded positively to the general population of midcentury England. According to the statistics presented, the typical inmate has a mean and median age of forty years; has an even chance of being male or female; has 2.2 children; is probably literate; and has a stated occupation, probably in the trades or in labor. This portrait, statistically drawn, does not present the face of the "great unwanted."

Alongside the social control theory stand three other sociological theories explaining the prevalence of mental disorder in the lower classes of society. A brief review of these other theories is in order. The "societal reaction hypothesis" suggests that "part of what is seen as psychiatric disorder among lower class people is actually their social class characteristics."[38] This theory, as well as the others, is of recent origin and was developed to explain the concentration of mental illness in lower-class Americans since 1950. Sociologists apply this theory, as well as the others—including social control—to historical data. The "societal reaction hypothesis" suggests that higher-class people judge lower-class people by their own standards of behavior. "This is a reflection of the large proportion [present day] of middle-class people who enter the mental health field and in turn project their own attitudes and class-based values into their evaluations of who is mentally ill."[39]

"The social stress hypothesis" suggests that the miserable living conditions of the lower classes generate stress, which in turn fosters psychiatric impairment.[40] The following statement suggests that this may be the case in present-day American society:

> The social stress explanation is plausible in light of the finding that the most disadvantaged members of the lower class have the greatest

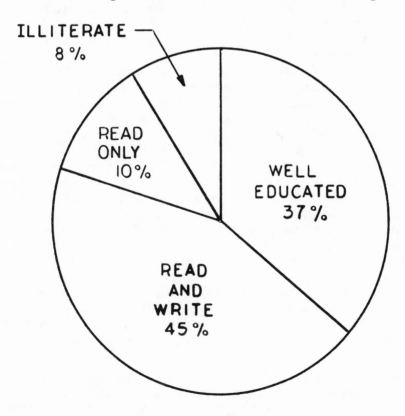

ILLITERATE — 8%

READ ONLY 10%

WELL EDUCATED 37%

READ AND WRITE 45%

Fig. 8. Literacy of Bethlehem Inmates, 1848

degree of impairment; blacks and Puerto Ricans, for example, common objects of discrimination in the United States, are more frequently and severely impaired than their lower-class Irish peers.[41]

This observation could be the result of racism, or at the very least
overt discrimination rather than poverty alone. We have no way of
knowing whether these causes were in effect in mid-nineteenth-
century England, except to note that very few "non-English"
persons were present in the asylum population studied. Another
researcher, David Mechanic,[42] suggests conversely that the lower-
class person may not only be equal to his higher-class counterparts, but may in fact be superior in dealing with stress. Mechanic
finds it more challenging to try to discover why so many lower-
class persons do so well in facing adversity, rather than why some
fail.

"The social selection hypothesis" is the opposite of the social
stress theory. This theory, also known as the "drift hypothesis,"
suggests that social class is not a cause but a consequence of
mental disorder. Although somewhat Darwinian in its hypothesis, this theory deserves some attention. According to this theory, the mentally ill person is likely to be a member of the lower
class because his disorder prevented him from functioning at a
higher-class level; consequently, he became downwardly mobile
and "drifted" into the lower class.[43] The studies made based upon
this theory all employ the same logic; if the parents of mentally
disordered persons are in a higher social class than the mentally
ill person, then the mental disorder preceded social class.[44] One
research team in 1972 studied the social class of fathers of mental
patients in Great Britain. They found that the social class of the
fathers did not differ from the general population, but the patients
were often downwardly mobile.[45] In our study, we find that this
could be the case with domestic servant girls between the ages of
twenty and twenty-nine who rank in the labor/service category of
our study. Not surprisingly, 65 percent of these girls were committed by parents of the next higher social class (trades and
clerical). However, we suggest that rather than "social selection"
as the cause of their downward mobility, the social drift had more
to do with their employment possibilities and/or their marriage
possibilities. It is even possible that the drift downward led to
their mental condition.

> It seems that, for every study supporting the social stress model, there
> is another verifying the social selection (drift theory) model. This is
> not surprising because the two models are not mutually exclusive;

class can determine illness in one case and illness can determine class in another.[46]

We must keep in mind that these four sociological theories—social control, societal reaction, social stress, and social selection (drift theory)—are present-day constructs dealing with present-day situations, not historical theories based on historical research. With the exception of the downwardly mobile servant girls, we find no statistical evidence to support any of these constructs in the present study. Although each may be plausible in the abstract—social stress is an appealing one—we find statistical evidence inadequate to support the social control theory. As suggested previously, the inmate population of this study corresponds positively to the general population.[47]

The analysis of the statistical frequency and cross-tabulations of the authority by which the inmate population was committed is presented in Figure 9. (It should be noted that until 1862 it was unlawful for a patient to commit himself.) Scull contends that most families sought to avoid the label "pauper" and the stigma that accompanied it. Pride was more important than pocketbooks.[48] A comparison of the inmate social class group as it relates to the admitting authority shows that pride did not deter the labor or trades group from committing their own family members to asylums. Within the trades group, of those persons committed by their spouse (60.7 percent), twice as many wives were committed by their husbands as husbands by wives. This is only true of the trades category of social class. Interestingly, of the parent-committed patients, there were no admissions from the classes of wealth, professional, or dregs—only the trades and labor groups. Of the parent-committed group, most (48.3 percent) were in the labor group, followed closely by the trades group (45.2 percent). Within the admitting authority category that can be regarded as family, the great majority committed were within the labor/service social class group. Pride does not appear to have been a deterrent in the admitting process. Admission by the authority of Her Majesty meant court-declared admission under pauper status as opposed to the criminal admissions that came under the admitting authority of the secretary of state. Although 88.6 percent of Her Majesty's admissions were of the social group deemed dregs, persons from the labor, trades, and professional groups also presented themselves to the court to obtain pauper status and subsequent asylum admission. This would suggest that persons did in fact declare themselves paupers for the express purpose of obtain-

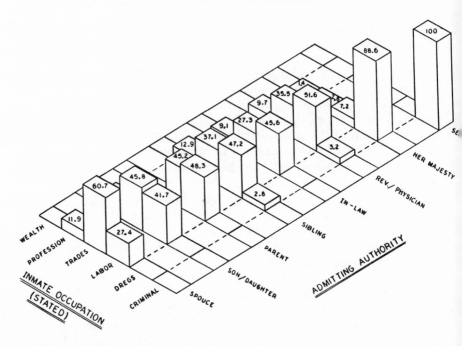

Fig. 9. Admitting Authority

ing treatment. There is no way to determine how many of the other admissions acted in the same manner—declaring pauper status to receive care.

Statistical frequencies and cross-tabulations were compiled and analyzed on the diagnosis and cause of illness among the case histories used in this study. We must keep in mind that the physical/moral causes of the nineteenth century correspond to what we refer to today as biogenic (organic) and environmental: "Today there are two major schools of thought in terms of etiological perspective: the biogenic and the environmental. These are roughly equivalent to the somatogenic (physical) and psychogenic (moral) labels used in earlier periods."[49] Table 2 shows the causes listed for the disorders diagnosed in the study population. With the exception of masturbation,[50] we can see that the physical causes listed relate favorably to what we would today call biogenic (organic) and the moral causes listed relate to the present-day use of environmental.

A breakdown of the causes of illness as compared to sex (Figure 10) shows that a total of 61 percent of all causes were described as physical and 39 percent were described as moral. Of the physical causes of illness, 53 percent were ascribed to males and 47 percent to females. Of the moral causes of illness, 42 percent were ascribed to males and 58 percent to females. The male/female split hovers too close to the fiftieth percentile to draw any conclusions about the physical and moral categories having sexist overtones.

The primary diagnoses made in our statistical sample included mania, monomania, dementia, melancholia, epilepsy, imbecility, and fear-anxiety. All except epilepsy, now recognized as a phys-

Table 2
Causes for Diagnosed Disorders

Physical Causes	Moral Causes
Puerperal	Grief
Intemperance of drink	Over-study
Critical period of life (menopause)	Reading of revelations
Protracted lactation	Embarrassed circumstances
Over-exertion	Loss in business
Bodily illness	Ill treatment (abused)
Fever: typhus, scarlet, rheumatic, yellow	Anxiety
Diarrhea	Disappointed affections
Weather (excessive heat, etc.)	Domestic troubles
Sensual excess	Want of employment
Blow on head	Love
Debility	Religion
Childbearing	Fright
Suppressed menses	Desertion
Suckling	Change of residence (rural to urban)
Hemorrhage	Sudden change from quiet to bustle
Brain fever	Vexation
Uterine disturbance	Jealousy
Head injury	Seduction
Severe bee stings	Study of astrology
Influenza	Reverse of fortune
Neuralgia	Consulting a fortune teller
Itch	Attending socialist lectures
Ulceration	Imprisonment
Cough	False accusation
Paralysis (syphilis)	Political enthusiasm
Constipation	Gambling
Masturbation	Solitude
Senility	Poverty
	Disgrace

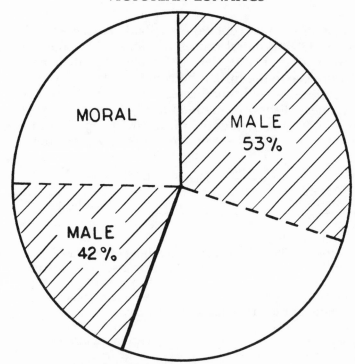

Fig. 10. Cause of Illness Breakdown by Sex

ical illness, and fear-anxiety are today called psychoses. It was recognized that epilepsy had a strongly physical cause, while fear-anxiety (today called a neurosis not a psychosis) was recognized as not as severe an illness as the others and was seen to have a high expectation for cure. The difference between today's terms of psychosis and neurosis is that the psychotics suffer a real break with reality and do not realize that they are disturbed. The neurotic realizes that he has a problem, and does not suffer a break with reality except in his distorted sense of impending doom. Most psychiatrists today assume that neurosis is environmental in origin—this corresponds to the high incidence of moral causation listed for the fear-anxiety syndrome in the study sample. Similarly, epilepsy was always listed as having a physical cause. Even this degree of accuracy among nineteenth-century diagnosticians is surprising given the state of the science of psychiatry.

A comparison of the initial diagnosis made by the admitting physician (Figure 11) shows that mania accounts for 47 percent of the total, dementia accounts for 17 percent, and monomania 3 percent. These three disorders, with a total of 67 percent of all disorders, are collectively called schizophrenia today. Melancholia, depression in modern terminology, accounts for 25 percent of the total, and epilepsy, imbecility, and fear-anxiety make the combined total of 8 percent.

The symptoms associated with schizophrenia today are strikingly similar to the symptoms attributed to mania, monomania,

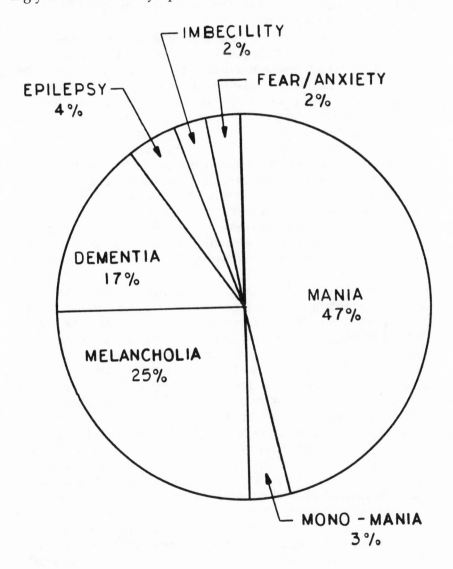

Fig. 11. Disorder/Diagnosis Breakdown

and dementia in the mid-nineteenth century. According to Gallagher, schizophrenia is mainly expressed through disordered thoughts, difficulty in communication and interpersonal relationships, and problems in reality testing. As a result of these difficulties, the schizophrenic withdraws from social interaction and retreats into his private reality. "In addition to these common features, there are more specific symptoms commonly known as the 'four A's of schizophrenia.' "[51]

The first A describes the symptoms ascribed to dementia in the nineteenth century. The first A of schizophrenia is an "affective" disturbance, which is observed as a flatness of personality that shows very little outward display of emotion. When emotion is displayed, it is often inappropriate—such as laughing when describing a tragedy. The second A describes the symptoms ascribed to monomania in the nineteenth century. The second A of modern schizophrenia is "autism." This term refers to an extremely self centered manner of thinking, which is also filled with fantasy. The third and fourth A's describe the symptoms ascribed to mania in the nineteenth century. The third A of the modern theory is an "association of ideas," which lacks continuity. One cannot move in a logical fashion from one group of thoughts to another. The fourth A is "ambivalence," which refers to taking two diametrically opposed emotions toward the same thing, or person, at the same time.[52]

One theory of schizophrenia holds that the disorder is the result of belonging to the poorest socioeconomic class. Some researchers believe that being poor may in itself cause the illness. Poor people frequently experience very stressful existences—broken homes, lack of educational oportunities, inability to achieve cultural goals (home ownership, for example), and degrading treatment by others.[53] The desire to escape these stressful conditions could therefore cause a lower-class person to break with reality in search of relief from the miserable conditions of a deprived life.[54] Although, again, this theory is of recent origin, the present study revealed that most of the dregs (81 percent) suffered from mania; the laboring class was overrepresented (70 percent) in the dementia diagnosis; monomania was, however, a distinctly higher-social-class illness (93 percent). These three nineteenth-century disorder diagnoses—mania, dementia, and monomania—make up the modern-day diagnostic term of schizophrenia. It appears that, with the exception of monomania, the theory of a concentration in the lower classes was as possible in mid-nineteenth-century England as it is in present-day America. Any of the previously mentioned social theories could be plausible explanations for this occurrence, the social stress and the drift theories being the most attractive.

Of the disorder/diagnoses studied in the present sample, we find a near-even male/female split among the sufferers of mania and monomania (Figure 12). Dementia, at 62 percent male, shows underrepresentation among females, whereas melancholia is overrepresented among females at 62 percent. Epilepsy shows a near-even male/female split, whereas imbecility, at 66 percent male, shows a decided male tendency. Fear-anxiety (a neurosis, not a psychosis—commonly called a nervous breakdown today) is decidedly female oriented at 63 percent.

The female diagnosis rate (62 percent) within the disorder melancholia corresponds with the rate in present-day studies. One researcher found this psychosis to occur three times more frequently among women than among men.[55] It was also found that the condition occurs most frequently in women between fifty-one and sixty years of age.[56] Our study sample corresponds in that the highest incidence is in the age group between forty and sixty-one and the greater majority (66 percent) were between forty and forty-nine. Below the age of forty and above the age of sixty-one the rates dropped significantly. The major symptom of melancholia is severe depression with some paranoia.

> The overriding factor in the etiology of melancholia in both men and women, is the recognition that the zenith of life has passed and earlier ambitions are not likely to be achieved. Combined with this is institutional prejudice against the aging person. This phenomenon, known as ageism, takes the form of stereotyping, mythmaking, distaste, and/or avoidance of the aging person.[57]

Women appear to suffer more from melancholia in the middle years due to menopause (called "critical period of life" by nineteenth-century diagnosticians). Although menopause may cause some biological dysfunction, the sociocultural theorists today suggest that it is more likely that some women react to menopause with depression because of the limited definition of the female sex role in American culture.

> If women have based their lives on a narrow range of fulfilling experiences, such as childbearing and childrearing, they have no alternative channels through which to gain satisfaction when childbearing is no longer possible. They feel then at menopause that they have lost their only function in society, and depression is the result.[58]

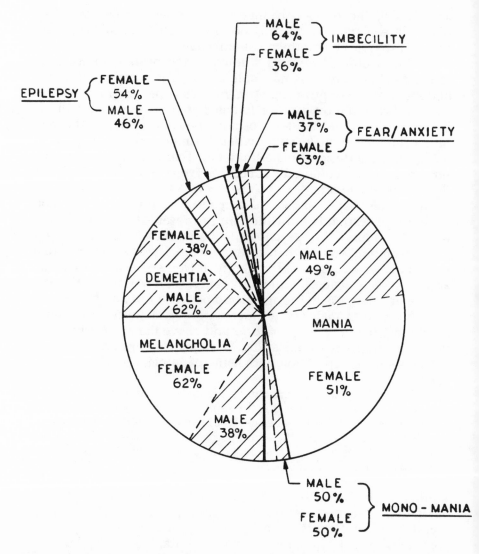

Fig. 12. Disorder/Diagnosis by Sex Breakdown

These present day American theories may have some validity as applied to our study. The majority of women diagnosed as suffering from melancholia listed no occupation and 55 percent were ascribed as a moral cause of illness.

The moral/physical etiological breakdown among the disorders/diagnoses of the study sample (Figure 13) shows that mania,

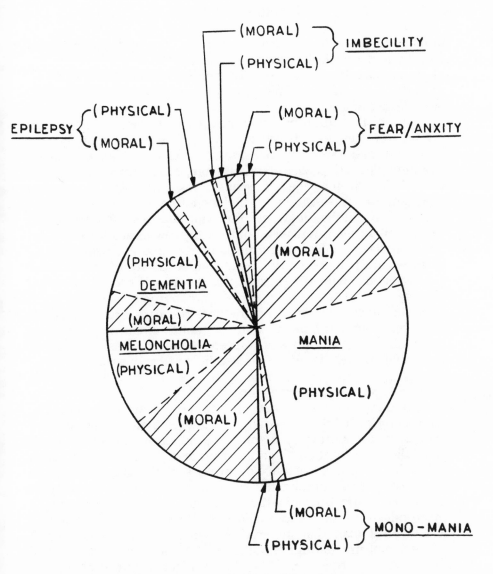

Fig. 13. Disorder by Cause (Moral/Physical) Breakdown

monomania, and melancholia are nearly evenly split between morally and physically attributed causes. Dementia is decidedly physical in its discerned cause, as is epilepsy and imbecility. Fear-anxiety has an overwhelming morally attributed cause, as would be expected of a neurosis.

A few of the moral causes attributed to the fear-anxiety syndrome were religious frustration, grief, overstudy, money worries, reduced circumstances, and vexation. These causes, although cloaked in Victorian language, are familiar elements to us in the syndrome called "nervous breakdown."

Among the causes given for melancholia besides critical period of life were childbearing, suckling, and suppressed menses; obviously all apply to females. Some of the causes attributed to the melancholia of males were grief, adverse circumstances, money worries, and responsibility. The attributed causes of melancholia are in keeping with the present-day theories of causation of this illness.

In summary, we can conclude that the construct of medical oppression, utilizing moral management as an aid to incarcerate huge numbers of society's unwanted, is a myth. This construct of the social control theorists[59] is invalidated by the statistical evidence.

With regard to the statement that "moral treatment actively sought to transform the lunatic into something approximating the bourgeois ideal,"[60] the evidence suggests that this manner of treatment was genuinely inspired by humanitarianism. To suggest otherwise would disregard the professed goals of the reformers and assume a consistency of purpose that runs counter to the pluralism present among the reformers themselves. To suggest otherwise would also deny the therapeutic optimism experienced by both lay-reformers and medical practitioners alike. The biological view of man that inspired the physiological psychological paradigm of mental illness blended with the humanitarian ideal of humane treatment and the theory of environmental (moral) causation to produce the moral management of the insane. Moral causation of the mid-nineteenth century corresponds to present-day views of environmental determinism as a source of mental illness, not the semantically misinterpreted immorality of the inmate population.

The allegation that the moral managers sought to bring the mentally ill in line with a bourgeois ideal can be challenged but not statistically refuted. The myth of the "great unwanted," however, is clearly invalid, at least for this sample. This study presents no statistical evidence to support the sociological theories of societal reaction or social stress; it did find some slight evidence of the social drift theory. Only negative evidence of the social control theory was apparent in the study sample. The typical inmate had an even chance of being male or female, an average age of forty years, 2.2 children, and a stated occupation prior to becoming ill. Midcentury England apparently felt that such a life was not expendable and therefore not "unwanted." According to an urban development study on nineteenth-century London, sanitary reform sprang from a respect for life.

> The movement for sanitary reform sprang not from an aesthetic revulsion against urban conditions or from disinterested philanthropy, but from an attitude briefly expressed by Lord Shaftesbury as "There is nothing so economical as humanity." Lack of adequate sanitary facilities in towns . . . resulted in high urban death rate and periodic scourges of epidemic disease. It was this waste of life, a valuable national resource, which provided the spur to change.[61]

If the midcentury Victorians saw life as a valuable resource, it would hardly follow that a person in midlife, with a small family and an occupation in the trades or labor, would be "dumped" because he was not useful to society, unless he actually was believed to be ill.

Alternate explanations exist concerning the presence of large numbers of persons, many of them paupers, in the institutions at midcentury. Although some will be detailed in length in the conclusion, we may suggest here that a number of declared paupers may have only declared such status for the purpose of admission for treatment in a county asylum. The committing-authority statistics show that pride was not a major family deterrent.

With regard to the diagnosed disorder and supposed cause of illness reported in this study, we find that most diagnoses were made in the category that we now call schizophrenia. In view of recent studies showing the prevalence of this disorder among the lower classes of American society, it is possible that the disease determined the social class makeup within the Victorian asylum— a large number with this disorder belong to the laboring class. This conclusion, however, lacks statistical validity and is offered here only as a possibility. Rather, the alternate theory presented in the next chapter is one that deals with a general bureaucratic revolution in government, including asylum development. The present study does show statistical evidence that the study population's diagnoses correlate favorably to diagnoses made today. This either speaks well for the mad-doctors of the Victorian era, or poorly for our own psychiatric community.

In short, in view of the evidence gathered in the course of this study, social control of the lunatic community in mid-nineteenth-century England appears to be a myth.

6

THE DEVELOPMENT OF CENTRALIZED BUREAUCRACY

The Growth of Government Debate—An Alternate Theory

> I know, and all the world knows, that revolutions never go backward.
>
> —William Henry Seward, 1858

The evidence presented thus far in this study has shown that the social control theory of the vast institutionalization of the insane is not valid for England in the mid-nineteenth century. An alternate theory to the one the social control theorists present can, however, be discerned in the general bureaucratic expansion experienced in England during that era.

State intervention into previously local or private-sector activities that led to centralization of government took many forms. This study discussed at length the interventionist activity surrounding the development of the asylum within the social-service delivery system. Other examples that describe the process and show the results of centralization can be seen in the regulatory legislation, such as the factory reform and safety regulations in the coal mine, and in institutional reform, such as in the army. These examples will be expanded in this chapter. However, to put these examples, as well as the example of asylum development, into the context of a theoretical model—the discovery of a social evil, leading to inquiry, and then to subsequent legislation to remedy the social evil—it becomes necessary to set forth such a model. The model was developed by Oliver MacDonagh and became the center of a debate between MacDonagh and Henry Parris as to the nature of the growth of government in nineteenth-century England.

It cannot be seriously doubted that the level of government

activity rose during the reign of Victoria. George Watson has argued:

> The process was cumulative, undesigned as a totality, and beleaguered by a widespread suspicion of paternalism and centralization of power. If the argument about the rival merits of local and central power tended increasingly to be resolved in favor of central government, that was less on doctrinaire grounds than for reasons of administrative convenience.[1]

Many historians, led in this theory by MacDonagh, have argued that nineteenth-century England experienced a "revolution in government." "Revolution," in this case, is used to describe unprecedented growth in central-government intervention into previously local administration. Other historians, led by Parris, have acknowledged bureaucratic growth, but contend it was not "revolutionary." MacDonagh might have avoided some of the criticism leveled against his work had he entitled it "the revolution in administration," rather than "the revolution in government."[2] The "traditional distinction that is made between 'politics' and 'administration' is a distinction between the setting of goals and the carrying-out of activities to reach these goals."[3] The most important part of MacDonagh's work, however, is the model that he establishes. Although the merits of the model have not been seriously challenged, the debate surrounding the theory is worth exploring in detail.

Any discussion of the "revolution in government" debate must begin with an appraisal of A. V. Dicey's work *Law and Opinion in England*, for all subsequent theorists have either disputed or augmented various aspects of Dicey's conclusions. Although originally written in 1905, this work is still considered first in the field and "the best introduction to the interplay between thought and political action in the period since 1832."[4]

Dicey's first thesis was that "the beliefs or sentiments which during the nineteenth-century have governed the development of the law have in strictness been public opinion, for they have been the wishes and ideas as to legislation held by the people of England."[5] His subsequent conclusion was that the nineteenth century could be divided into three distinct periods, "during each of which a different current or stream of opinion was predominant, and governed the development of the law of England."[6] Dicey's chronological divisions begin with the "Period of Old Toryism or Legislative Quiescence (1800–1830),"[7] which he sees as a period of stagnation. The second division, "The Period of Benthamism or Individualism (1825–1870),"[8] is described as one of utilitarian reform associated with the ideas of Jeremy Bentham. The third and final division is the "Period of Collectivism (1865–1900),"[9] described as an era of energetic state intervention. Dicey concludes his chronological divisions:

> The difference in the spirit of the three great currents of opinion may be thus summarized: Blackstonian toryism was the historical reminiscence of paternal government; Benthamism is a doctrine of law reform; collectivism is a hope of social regeneration. Vague and inaccurate as this sort of summary must necessarily be, it explains how it happened that individualism under the guidance of Bentham affected, as did no other body of opinion, the development of English Law.[10]

It is Dicey's assumption of Bentham's influence on mid-nineteenth-century legislation that absorbs his opponents. Often, the dispute centers around Dicey's idea that utilitarianism and laissez-faire existed simultaneously.[11] In addition, Dicey's chronological divisions came under attack in the subsequent debate.

The dispute opened with the publication in 1958 of an article by Oliver MacDonagh titled "The Nineteenth-Century Revolution in Government: A Reappraisal." MacDonagh borrowed the term "revolution" to describe fundamental change from G. R. Elton's work *The Tudor Revolution in Government*,[12] which alluded to a similar occurrence in the sixteenth century. Both Elton and Mac-Donagh have been criticized for their use of the term, if by that term is meant a complete overthrow of an existing order. Mac-Donagh, however, contends that although

> this revolution has not the standing of its industrial and agrarian cousins . . . most historians take it for granted that the function and structure of government changed profoundly in the course of the nineteenth century . . . and would probably agree, moreover, that this change was revolutionary in a sense in which the changes of the seventeenth and eighteenth centuries, or even that of the first half of the twentieth century, were not; and also that it was revolutionary both in kind and quantity.[13]

MacDonagh gave Dicey his due by terming *Law and Opinion* a "great book," before revealing that "other merits apart . . . it is the work of a lawyer and a student of political ideas, not that of an historian; and whatever else we find there, we shall not find a 'history' of the change in the nature of the state."[14] He suggests that Dicey "intellectualizes" the problem by not making it clear that the process of centralization was not a conscious one. In that context MacDonagh offers an alternative theory, contending that, although external influences such as prevailing currents of thought, industrialization, population growth, concentration and mobility, and concomitant social problems had an influence, the primary impetus for centralization of government function was internal and organic, and involved a self-sustaining and self-propelling momentum.[15]

MacDonagh then suggested a five-stage development process to explain the "revolution in government." The first stage proposed that the exposure of a social evil led to prohibitory legislation. "Men's instinctive reaction was to legislate the evil out of existence."[16] The second stage was reached when special officers were appointed to enforce the new laws. These officers accumulated information on the nature of the specific social evil that they were empowered to investigate and report upon, and this knowledge quickly led to the demand for further legislation .[17] Stage three commenced when the officers demanded a clearly defined supervising central body and culminated when centralization was in place.[18] The fourth stage saw a dynamic concept of administration take the place of a static one and the gradual crystallization of the idea of administrative expertise. The officers then "ceased to regard their problems as resolvable once and for all by some grand piece of legislation or by the multiplication of their own numbers," but instead saw the answer in their own expertise gained by continuing experience and experiment.[19] The fifth and final stage was reached when administrative officers secured legislation "which awarded them discretion not merely in the application of its clauses but even in imposing penalties and framing regulations."[20]

In many aspects of MacDonagh's model, such as his concept of internal and organic organizational growth, the concepts conform to accepted modern organizational theory. The concept of "negative entropy," for example, states that an organization has the capacity of self-renewal; it is not limited by the participation of or the life expectancy of any individual within it. This concept suggests that the officers who were appointed to carry out legislative enactments designed to counteract a social evil lost their individual identities within a group identity that had self-generating potential. MacDonagh also, perhaps unknowingly, employs another accepted concept of organizational theory—that of "empire building." A first and fundamental source of power for administrative agencies is their ability to attract outside support. The support system required to maintain the existence of an agency must include public opinion, legislative reinforcement, and executive (centralized governing body) support. To sustain the life of an agency, support from the external environment must be solicited, political bases must be organized, jurisdiction and regulatory power must be increased, and public opinion must be curried by a show of knowledge or expertise. Unlike their counterparts in the private sector, government agencies cannot acquire power, and continued existence, by means of economic growth in the market place; rather, power must be initially developed and cultivated within the constraints of the governmental/political system. "Empire building" is the term used to describe the ongoing process of securing the necessary support to maintain the existence and continued growth of the agency.[21] We can see this concept in action in MacDonagh's theory and subsequent model.

Henry Parris's "The Nineteenth-Century Revolution in Government: A Reappraisal Reappraised," offered a rebuttal to MacDonagh's theories, and the debate was on.[22] Parris first commended MacDonagh on his attempt to develop a model with which to view the phenomenon of centralization rather than attacking institutions piecemeal with studies of each governmental agency. However, he criticized MacDonagh for not taking a more critical stand against Dicey. Parris contended that Dicey was misleading about the nineteenth-century revolution to begin with. Parris states that: "Dicey's purpose was not only to describe the consequences of radical Liberalism, but also, as a Whiggish exponent of the true Liberal faith, to denounce them."[23] Parris further suggests that Dicey's work stood in need of reexamination in the areas of his summary of Benthamism,[24] his summary of midcentury legislation, and, primarily, his division of the nineteenth century into periods.[25] Agreeing with MacDonagh that "any discussion of the nineteenth-century revolution in government must base itself on Dicey's work,"[26] he reexamines each of these areas and concludes that Dicey was inaccurate in many of his assumptions. Regarding Dicey's divisions of the century into three distinct periods, he states:

It may seem merely pedantic solemnly to consider whether Dicey was right in discerning three periods into which his subject could be divided. What can it matter, one may ask, whether there were three periods or only two—or for that matter, four? The question is of importance, however, because most of the distortions of his argument are closely bound up with his determination to demonstrate distinct trends in opinion and legislation.[27]

The real issue, as Parris sees it, is that by "forcing the second turning point" and calling it the "period of Benthamism or Individualism," Dicey begins the utilitarian–laissez-faire confusion, and Parris regards this as a "travesty of Benthamism."[28] Parris attributes this "travesty" on Dicey's part to Dicey's Whiggish view, because "Dicey's career as a political partisan is of the greatest relevance to understanding his thought. An Orthodox Liberal until 1885, he broke with his party over Home Rule, and devoted much time and effort thenceforth as a speaker and pamphleteer to combating the doctrines and measures of his former associates."[29]

Parris, having pointed out what he believed to be the weaknesses in Dicey's argument, which he sees as perpetuating the myth that between 1820 and 1870 central control in England was under the influence of Bentham's individualistic ideas, concludes that MacDonagh's paper was of importance, even though it overlooked the false conclusions arrived at by Dicey and accepted by MacDonagh. "The importance of Dr. MacDonagh's paper," says Parris, "is that in it he offers such a framework" for studying the phenomenon of centralization via a model and that "it is a criticism of Dicey, in that it is based on assumptions which are inconsistent with the basic idea of *Law and Opinion*. Although Dr. MacDonagh does not explicitly criticize Dicey's views on many points, his own argument implies a rejection of them."[30]

Parris concludes his rebuttal with a model of his own, which he suggests will explain the nineteenth-century revolution in government while not succumbing to "the inherent difficulties of MacDonagh's model."[31] The model's stages are as follows: although in response to social and economic change, the nineteenth-century revolution in government cannot be understood without regard to contemporary thought about social and political organization; 1830 divides the nineteenth century into two periods with regard to the relationship between law and opinion; in the second period, after 1830, utilitarianism was the dominant current of opinion; the main principle of utilitarianism was "utility," which led to an increase both in laissez-faire and state intervention—simultaneously; and, finally, the special officers, appointed to administer the law, played an extensive role in formulating further legislation that increased their own powers.[32] On the subject of Bentham, Parris asserts that "it would be absurd to argue that Bentham revolutionized the British system of government by power of abstract thought alone. His ideas were influential because they were derived from the processes of change going on around him. He was working with the grain. But it does not follow that the same solutions would have been reached had he never lived."[33] Parris, therefore, differs from MacDonagh in concluding that there was nothing inevitable or organic about the institutional response to change. Although differing from MacDonagh in that aspect, Parris does conclude that the nineteenth-century did experience a "revolution in government,"[34] which he defined as extensive bureaucratic growth.

The Bentham dispute had come full circle, from Dicey's pro-Bentham argument, to MacDonagh's avoidance of crediting Bentham, to Parris's pro-Bentham conclusion; there for a while the discussion rested. Succeeding writers on nineteenth-century government have tended to follow MacDonagh's line of argument, and it is this group of historians who have been pilloried by Jenifer Hart in her article "Nineteenth-Century Social Reform: A Tory Interpretation of History."[35] Hart states that:

> In explaining progress in nineteenth-century England, they [the Tories] belittle the role of men and ideas, especially the role of the Benthamites; they consider that opinion, often moved by a Christian conscience, was generally humanitarian; that social evils were therefore attacked and dealt with when people felt them to be intolerable; that many changes were not premeditated or in some sense planned, but were the result of "the historical process" or of "blind forces."[36]

In this, she implies that social progress will not, in the future as in the past, take place without human effort. The pro-Bentham cause rose again. D. Roberts, in his article "Jeremy Bentham and the Victorian Administrative State," repeated MacDonagh's effort to limit the influence of Bentham;[37] Hart, conversely, extends Parris's comments on it and contends that "it is surely nearer the truth to hold that ideas can influence people who are unconscious of their origin, by becoming part of the general climate of opinion."[38] Hart also emphasizes the need to remember the empirical nature of the Benthamite approach.[39] Thus the case for Bentham is made again. The pro and con argument has gone on with little variation until the present.

The second part of the debate has centered around the development of executive discretions and delegated legislation (state intervention) against and parallel with some sort of laissez-faire concept. Arthur J. Taylor, in his work *Laissez-faire and State Intervention in Nineteenth-Century Britain*,[40] makes the profound observation that much of the dispute lies in an inadequate and frequently confused definition of laissez-faire. According to Taylor, the term originated in eighteenth-century France, but was not frequently found in British literature or debate before the middle of the nineteenth century.[41]

Taylor also suggests that time can obscure the meaning of a word, and that few who use the term laissez-faire in the present era can define it. Its meaning, therefore, can only be inferred. "There are some who would equate laissez-faire with anarchy," says Taylor, "while at the other extreme there are those who use it to mean no more than a preference for private rather than public enterprise. More frequently, laissez-faire has been used as a convenient shorthand for the general prescriptions of the Classical economists and in particular for a belief in the efficacy of a free market economy."[42] He also suggests that when applying the term to the nineteenth century, it is often used to imply central-government action to differentiate that action from local-government action as well as from private or corporate action. While some regarded local concern for public health as a move away from laissez-faire, others viewed resistance to the General Board of Health as a continuation of the laissez-faire principle. "Given these variations in definition, it is hardly surprising that one man's laissez-faire is another man's intervention."[43]

Bentham, of course, is central to much of the controversy about laissez-faire and state intervention, as was previously noted. Dicey found a direct association between Bentham and the concept of laissez-faire when he asserted that "laissez-faire was practically the most vital part of Bentham's legislative doctrine."[44] Twenty years after Dicey, Keynes implied a similar identification when he argued that "the language of the economist lent itself to the laissez-faire interpretation. But the popularity of the doctrine must be laid at the door of the political philosophers, whom it happened to suit, rather than of the political economists."[45] C. R. Fay in his work *Great Britain from Adam Smith to the Present Day* made a distinction between the attitude of the utilitarians to economic questions where "the will of the manufacturers and the abstract laws of political economy" were to be given play, and their attitude to social questions "where a measure of paternalistic control by the state was required."[46] "This distinction pointed the way towards an increasing realization on the part of historians of the tendencies towards collectivism inherent in the Benthamite philosophy."[47] By 1948, J. B. Brebner in his article "Laissez-faire and State Intervention in Nineteenth-Century Britain" went so far as to assert that "Bentham was the archetype of British collectivism."[48] Taylor makes the point, however, that a distinction must be made between Bentham and the Benthamites, a distinction he feels is often overlooked by historians.

> Benthamism—Utilitarianism—Philosophic Radicalism, the multiplicity of names emphasises the point—was not a highly developed body of rigid doctrine held in common by a tightly-knit and severely disciplined sect. Those who were called Benthamites were united in a shared respect for Bentham himself, in a common belief in the validity of the greatest happiness principle as a guide to social policy and action, and in a commitment to reason as the key to good government.[49]

Dicey had pointed out that "utilitarianism thus comprehended could in time be made the basis for many varied policies and systems spanning the entire spectrum from extreme laissez-faire to an all-embracing collectivism."[50] As long as Bentham was alive, the movement had a unity of action as well as of basic principle, but "after his death, its centrifugal characteristics became increasingly apparent in the lives of men so distinguished but so diverse as Edwin Chadwick, George Grote and the Younger Mill."[51]

With regard to periodization, after 1830 (the era termed individualistic—implied laissez-faire—by Dicey), in the face of the increasing problems presented by industrialization, population growth, and urbanization, the interventionist implications of the Benthamite philosophy increasingly asserted themselves. An example of this, according to Taylor, is provided by the policies of Edwin Chadwick.[52]

That the intervention was social rather than economic, in the sense of laissez-faire, argument has been carried a stage further by David Roberts in his work *The Victorian Origins of the British Welfare State*.[53] Roberts sees in Victorian governmental activities "the first beginnings of the Welfare State which is today a distinguishing feature of the British Government."[54] It is the pursuit of the same theme that prompted Phyllis Deane in *The First Industrial Revolution* to state:

> The odd thing was that a revolution in government which represented the beginnings of collectivism and of the modern welfare state should have taken place in a community whose articulate political prejudices

were flatly in opposition to such a development. It happened because of the existence of strong underlying pressures which proved in the end irresistible. There were, for example, the ideological pressures associated with the spread of utilitarian doctrines amongst educated people. These looked on the face of them as though they were going to weaken the power of the state, for they were in close sympathy with Adam Smith's doctrine of the "invisible hand" and were constantly attacking the complicated and ineffective network of government regulations which characterized the traditional pre-industrial society. The real objective of the philosophical radicals, however, turned out to be not freedom from government but freedom from inefficient government.[55]

Intervention, according to this argument, was prompted not by any conviction of its innate desirability, but by the inescapable need to meet pressing problems, created largely by the twin forces of industrialization and urbanization, which were incapable of individualist or private-sector solutions. According to Deane, these underlying pressures ensured that "a generation reared in the doctrines of laissez-faire should systematically lay the foundations of modern collectivism."[56] The argument thus reaches its ultimate polarity, the age of laissez-faire coming face to face with the embryonic welfare state. However, as we have come to see, state intervention and laissez-faire were not mutually exclusive concepts.[57]

According to MacDonagh's model, social legislation can be broken down into a five-stage process: exposure of a social evil; appointment of special officers to investigate or enforce the remedy; insistence of the officers for a central supervisory body; gaining of expertise and special knowledge of the field by the officers; and, finally, securing further legislation, which awards the administrative officers regulating powers. This model at work can be seen in the examples of factory reform, coal mine safety reform, institutional reform within the army, and, central to the thesis of this study, mental health reform.

The first factory legislation was the Health and Morals Act of 1802.[58] It was inspired by epidemics in the late eighteenth century among the factory children, which prompted an investigation, a subsequent report, and finally the legislation itself.[59] The act addressed reform in three main areas. It limited the hours children could work; regulated the physical environment in which children could work; and required the education of working children. All three were radical and innovative.[60] However, no government was made responsible for its enforcement and its fate was avoidance. A popular campaign was mounted in response to the lack of enforcement, and in 1832 a Tory radical, Michael Sadler, a member of Parliament for Newark, introduced a ten-hours bill. In response, the manufacturers organized a powerful special-interest group in Parliament, which postponed the legislation by agreeing to the setting up of a select committee on child labor in textiles. When the evidence came in, it depicted a horrible system of abuses and some far-reaching action appeared to be inevitable.[61] One of the witnesses was an overseer who had been named in earlier evidence as one who was cruel to the working children. His testimony, in part, follows:

Q. Have you had much experience regarding the working of children in factories?
A. Yes, about twenty-seven years.

Q. Have you a family?
A. Yes, eight children.

Q. Have any of them gone to the factories?
A. All.

Q. At what age?
A. The first went at six years of age.

Q. State the effect upon your children?
A. Of a morning when they had to get up, they have been so fast asleep that I have had to go up stairs and lift them out of bed, and have heard their crying with feelings of a parent; I have been much affected by it.

Q. Were not they much fatigued at the termination of such a day's labour as that?
A. Yes, many times I have seen their hands moving while they have been nodding, almost asleep; they have been doing their business almost mechanically.

Q. While they have been almost asleep, they have attempted to work?
A. Yes, and they have missed the carding and spoiled the thread, when we have had to beat them for it.

Q. Could they have done their work towards the termination of such a long day's labour, if they had not been chastised to do it?
A. No.

Q. You think they could have kept awake till the seventeenth hour had they not been chastised?
A. No.

Q. Will you state what effect it had upon your children at the end of the day?
A. At the end of their day's work when they have come home, instead of taking their victuals in their hands, they have dropped asleep. And sometimes when we have sent them to bed with a little bread or something to eat in their hand, I found it in their bed the next morning.[62]

At the beginning of 1833, the ten-hours bill was reintroduced; it provided for children between the ages of nine and eighteen to work only ten hours daily and eight hours on Saturday. These regulations were to be enforced by compelling employers to keep time records.[63] The manufacturers retorted that expert economists had demonstrated that the ten-hours bill would ruin British industry by depriving it of its profits; the textile industry secured a postponement by agreeing to yet another investigation. The bill was due for a second reading just nine weeks after the investigating committee was set up, so an aura of haste surrounded the investigation. The investigating commission, dominated by Chadwick, outstripped the opposition by reducing the children's hours and at the same time enabling adult workers to work as long, or perhaps even longer, through the principle of the double shift.[64] The final form of the act decreed: no employment of children under nine years of age; no child under the age of thirteen was to work more than nine hours per day and each child was to receive two hours of schooling per day; no child under eighteen was to work more than twelve hours a day (excluding meal breaks); and inspectors were to be appointed by Parliament to enforce these provisions.[65] The appointment of inspectors, as in the Public Health Act and the Poor Law Reform, insured enforcement by the central authorities.

The major call for reform in the coal mines came from public demand derived from well-publicized accidents, which was not the case in the textile industry. Major opposition to mine reform was lodged in the House of Lords (mine ownership being a primarily aristocratic endeavor). Conversely, the House of Commons (the middle class being the main profiters of the textile industry) showed more opposition to factory reform than the upper chamber.[66] Safety in the mines had been a point of discussion and inquiry for many years before a select committee was set up in 1835. The evidence pointed clearly to a need for legislation, but contradictions of scientific opinion on safety methods delayed the committee from proposing legislation. The 1842 act came instead from concern for child labor in the mines. The addition of the exclusion of women from underground work came more from a moral concern for their half-nakedness than for their physical safety. But, the precedent made it easier to include them in future legislation.[67]

Thus, we again see an example of MacDonagh's initial model proposition at work—the discovery of a social evil—leading to inquiry and subsequent legislation. The first real impetus for the 1842 campaign came from the bishop of Norwich's speech. It was on his description of women and children "chained to their labour of dragging small vehicles loaded with coal through narrow apertures or passages, in which they were obliged to crawl upon their hands and knees, their garments drenched with water,"[68] that public attention riveted. The fight to secure legislation, however, was not as simple as MacDonagh's model would suggest. Lord Ashley, a Tory member of Parliament (later to become Lord Shaftesbury), had been responsible for the 1832 bill on factory legislation; now he became involved in composing and presenting a bill to terminate the horrible conditions in the mines. Commenting on the practices described by the bishop of Norwich, Ashley assumed that no one would argue that such practices could be tolerated in a civilized state.

> Never, I believe, since the first disclosure of the horrors of the African slave-trade, has there existed so universal a feeling on any one subject in this country, as that which now pervades the length and breadth of the land in abhorrence and disgust of this monstrous oppression of evils that are both disgusting and intolerable—disgusting they would be in a heathen country, and perfectly intolerable they are in one that professes to call itself Christian.[69]

The Commons gave in before such a declaration, unlike the Lords, "some of whose mine-owning members were made of sterner stuff."[70]

Ashley's early success with the Commons was met with opposition from the coal industry. Just as the textile factory owners had earlier based their opposition to the possible ruination of the industry, now the mine owners asserted that wholesale changes in the supply of labor would ruin their industry. Ashley attempted a compromise, which again passed the Commons, but was referred by the Lords to a select committee. The resultant act of 1842 was a badly mutilated version of the first proposals.[71] The act prohibited the employment of females of all ages and of boys under ten years of age, and the employment in machine-tending of all persons under the age of fifteen.[72] Though much compromised from Ashley's original proposal, the new Act embodied three great principles, two of them new to English law. These were the exclusion of certain persons from the management of machinery and the prohibition of child labor in a new field.[73]

The 1842 act contained an executive clause enabling the home secretary to appoint inspectors, but it was vague. Home Secretary Graham made only one appointment, that of H. S. Tremenheere as commissioner. Tremenheere was to serve sixteen years without either colleague or successor.[74] He reported annually on the social problems of the mining districts and undertook a few prosecutions, but his primary contribution was that he pressed for a new form of inspectorate as early as 1845. The subject of mine inspection came up in the Commons repeatedly between 1845 and 1850, but the bills were mainly derived from and supported only by radicals. The cry of class discrimination was raised. A radical member named Wakley observed "that whenever a measure to help the working classes was introduced it was staved off as long as possible. But if a noble Lord were blown out of a coal mine, there would be legislation on the subject the very next day the Parliament assembled."[75]

Mine disasters multiplied in the years 1847 to 1849, attracting more and more newspaper attention. Public opinion ran in favor of an inspectorate, and a Lord's select committee was appointed to investigate. The committee employed the help of two eminent scientists to investigate and report on various mine disasters. The scientists did establish causes, thereby lending the force of scientific authority to the pressures for reform begun by Tremenheere years earlier. The report of the select committee came out strongly in favor of some form of inspectorate;[76] the bill for it passed and received royal assent in August 1850.[77] The inspectors were empowered to enter any coal mine, examine its operations, and recommend changes where they judged procedures or machinery to be unsafe. If owners or managers refused to comply, the inspectors were to inform the home secretary; subsequent prosecution was assumed.[78] In November 1850, four inspectors were appointed to correlate with the four areas of inspection into which the country was divided. The inspection areas were, of course, much too large; each inspector had over four hundred collieries in his district.[79] In 1855 the number of inspectors grew to twelve—

still insufficient—but again the precedent of enforcement by central government of legislation devised to tackel a social ill was set.

As the inspectorate increased, mortality among miners decreased. In the decade 1851–60 the mortality rate from accidents among miners was 1 per 245 employed; in 1861–70 it was 1 per 300; and in 1871–75, 1 per 430.[80] Moreover, the fall in mortality was steepest in those classes of accident that the inspectors could do most to influence. Explosions accounted for 24 percent of the accident deaths in 1851–60 but only 17.8 percent in 1871–75. Conversely, deaths from roof and wall falls, which the inspectors could do least to check, rose from 37 to 41 percent of the totals over the same period.[81] By 1852 the inspectors had formed a corps that began to take on creative efforts as well as their regulatory obligations. In MacDonagh's view, which coincides with his theory of organic growth, the mine inspectorate began to develop internal momentum.[82] In the examples that we have described of factory and mine reform, we see the results and the process of centralization in regulatory legislation brought about by a social ill. In the next example we can view the same process taking place in an institutional setting.

According to Hew Strachan in his article "The Early Victorian Army and the Nineteenth-Century Revolution in Government,"[83] midcentury reform embodied all the manifestations of MacDonagh's model. First, Strachan suggests, an "intolerable situation" was created, largely through the press, which called for an inquiry over the massacre of the army in Afghanistan in the winter of 1841–42. This was the sort of crisis used to clinch their arguments about "intolerability."[84]

Although there were a number of royal commissions and select committees on the army, their impact was not as great as it appears to have been in other areas of reform. Part of the reason lies in the indifference of many members of Parliament to military matters and part is due to the fact that in the case of the army opposition to reform was conducted from within the administrative spectrum itself. This situation was only overcome by the presence of Wellington himself.[85] However slowly action came about, by 1854 reform or attempted reform in many areas can be found. Strachan enumerates:

The conditions of service of other ranks were changed out of all recognition: savings banks were established in 1842, cricket pitches laid out, five courts erected, and barrack libraries created. Prevention rather than punishment became the catchword, a system of good conduct awards was instituted in 1836, flogging was curtailed to fifty lashes in August 1846, compulsory education was introduced, and an attempt at limited enlistment was made.[86]

The reforming activity was also carried on in the areas of tactics and training. The adoption of the Minie rifle in 1851, followed by the Enfield rifle in 1853, gave every British soldier a weapon effective at 800 yards. Previous muskets only had a range of 150 yards. This technological innovation was followed by the opening of the Hythe school of musketry to train infantry in the use of more effective weaponry. Artillery also doubled in strength between 1851 and 1853.[87] Serious attempts were also made to consolidate military departments during these years, and by 1855 the principle consolidations were in place.

According to Strachan, this was the broad outline of army reform in the years that have been identified as those of greatest change in civilian administration. He asserts that "many of the same devices used in social reform can be found employed in military matters. The accumulation of statistics, until their weight presented an unanswerable argument for reform, so much a feature of Chadwick's assault on urban sanitary conditions, is also to be found in the army."[88] Again we see the process at work during the mid-nineteenth century—the identification of a problem; subsequent inquiry and resultant accumulation of evidence of a need for reform; and, finally, reform itself.

The development of the midcentury asylum also fits into the process of general bureaucratization of a social problem. Increasing awareness of the failure of the asylum system to provide adequate facilities led to the appointment of a Select Committee of the House of Commons in 1807. A social ill had been discovered. The 1807 Select Committee was charged with investigating the state of pauper lunatics. Investigation and data collection had begun. A report was issued by the 1807 committee, which led directly to the County Asylum Act of 1808. Further investigation and data collection led to the 1828 Madhouse Act, which provided for the establishment of a central commission to license and oversee asylums. A central supervisory body had been established. The 1834 Poor Law Amendment Act, however, created an alternate solution to the problem of poverty—the workhouse. A new social evil was detected—namely, that lunatics were detained in the workhouse rather than receiving special attention. More investigation began in light of the new social evil. In 1838 yet another select committee reported on the conditions endured by destitute lunatics in workhouses. The same year, the Metropolitan Commissioners (the central supervisory body) suggested further governmental intervention. The subsequent inspections, by the officers, resulted in a comprehensive report in 1844. The fourth criteria (assertion of administrative expertise) of Mac-Donagh's model has been met. By 1845 the fifth, and final, stage of MacDonagh's model was accomplished; administrative officers, and others such as Ashley, secured further legislation that awarded regulatory power to a centralized body and assured the attempt to remedy a social evil by the construction of asylums for the poor in every county throughout the country. Thus, we see the development of the midcentury asylum as fitting into a model designed to illuminate general bureaucratic growth. In this context, the development of the asylum does not take on proportions it does not deserve—that of social control.

What also must be recognized is that much of the bureaucratic growth of the era was unplanned and unintended. Many of the implicitly collectivist pieces of legislation and institutional reforms received little or no publicity at the time; others involved extraneous elements and conflicts of class or special interest that obscured the centralizing or collectivist implications. To obtain a clear understanding of the phenomenon one must realize that there was no coherent theory of collectivism until long after it had entered deeply if quietly into the system of state. It was a phenomenon without a head or a brain.

7

CONCLUSION

It is evident that the asylum developed within an expanding social-service delivery system, expected by and designed to benefit the inhabitants of England. By the end of the eighteenth century, it has become apparent that the private sector could not adequately fill the need for supervision and care of the insane. The establishment of a system of state-supported asylums became a reality only after thirty-eight years of investigation, debate, and discussion through a series of Select Committees begun in 1807. After more than two centuries of the most extreme localism, England was set in the direction of centralized government designed to deliver social services.

The Lunatics Act of 1845 made the erection of county and borough asylums compulsory. The money was to come from a general county tax and provisions were made for the central government to advance the money for the project to the county or borough. A central Lunacy Commission was established and these commissioners had the last word on all asylum matters.

The 1845 act remained, in substance, the fundamental determinant of provisions regarding lunatics until very late in the nineteenth century. During the period of this study and beyond, the demand for asylum space outstripped the supply. The progressive withdrawal of pauper lunatics from workhouses and private asylums swelled the numbers of the officially recognized insane and public asylums became overcrowded. This situation gave rise then and now to speculation as to why this happened. Theories proliferated to answer this question.

The social-service delivery system, the growth of which we traced in terms of the asylum, was but one element of increasing centralization of government and of growth in all societal aspects. The development of the health-care delivery system included the growth of the hospital system, and the development of a medical education criterion that led to the professionalization of physicians and the development of public health policies (including those for the sick poor),[1] which eventually grew into a National Health Service. The mid-nineteenth-century standards set by centralized government formed the basis for both the public and private health-care delivery systems. This shows yet another element of the influence of growing social needs upon an increasingly centralized provider—the centralized governmental bureaucracy.

The growth of centralized bureaucracy was traced in chapter 6. The "revolution in government" debate was outlined in an attempt to illuminate the dimensions of this change and the dynamics of institutional growth. The fact that government activity increased sharply during the reign of Victoria is indisputable. A centralized bureaucracy designed to carry out legislation experienced an equally rapid growth. Factory legislation and mine safety legislation led to an inspectorate that required a bureaucratic backup. The investigative and reforming tendency of the era was even evident in the army. In short, governmental interventionist activities spurred institutional growth in all societal aspects on a previously unknown scale.

The growth of science was traced and the change in the psychological paradigm documented in an attempt to add depth to the thesis that growth and change was the order of the day in many disparate areas of human endeavor. The nineteenth century was an era of growth, change, development, and excursion into unknown areas of experience. It is within this context that asylum growth must be viewed.

A startling social phenomenon of the nineteenth century was the sharp and steady rise in the proportion of the population officially recognized as insane and subsequently institutionalized. In 1807, according to a report of a parliamentary Select Committee, the incidence of insanity was 2.26 cases in every 10,000 of the general population;[2] by 1844 the number of insane had risen to 12.66 cases per 10,000,[3] a sixfold increase. By 1890 the number of insane per 10,000 increased to 29.63.[4] This increase and the disparity between private and pauper lunatics has given rise to a number of causation theories. "Between 1844 and 1860 the number of pauper lunatics increased by 96%."[5] Why was the increase so disproportionate between these two types of patients?

The commissioners on lunacy were disturbed by these increases and attempted an explanation that "the large number of cases previously unreported, have only recently been brought under observation."[6] This answer has never been satisfactorily refuted, while others of more recent origin have been suggested.

The social control theory is the one that this study is able to challenge statistically. As previously stated, the inmate population corresponded positively to the general population. The typical asylum inmate had an even chance of being male or female, had an average age of forty years, had 2.2 children, was most probably literate, and typically possessed a stated occupation in the trades or labor class.

Although the social control theory has been found to be statistically invalid, the question still remains: Why was there the large increase in asylum inmates? Andrew Scull has suggested yet another explanation, that "from the moment of their existence, asylums reduced people's level of tolerance of deviants. Given that an institutional remedy was available, people were no longer willing to put up with lunatic relatives."[7] Although this probably did happen in some cases, the empirical basis for motivational behavior is slender, and the limited evidence is contradictory.

> Observers of working-class behavior during the Cotton Famine, for instance, emphasize a willingness by kin and neighbours to help the worse-off with no hope of a return; and as Alan Ainsworth recently remarked, "above all, in an age when the working class had by necessity to turn inwards for relief to that mutuality and self-help basic to their communities . . . the Christian thing to do was to offer help and support in times of crisis to one's friends, workmates, neighbors, and especially to one's family."[8]

The question of what caused the rise in the numbers of institutionalized insane can perhaps best be answered after all by the contemporaries themselves:

> The passage of Ashley's acts (1845) ushered in a period of optimism in regard to the treatment of the insane. In the thirty years prior to 1845 the scattered efforts of small numbers of philanthropists and medical men had brought about striking improvements in the condition of asylums and the care of patients. With the powers and resources of the state now behind the movement it is little wonder that most lunacy reformers faced the future with confidence. Their expectations were perhaps best expressed by the lunacy commissioners in 1847: "The present humane method of treating the insane and the provision made, at the public cost, for Pauper Lunatics, of Asylums furnished with every comfort . . . promise to diminish the numbers of the permanently insane and cannot fail to alleviate, in a great degree, the suffering of the most afflicted class of human beings."[9]

However, by the 1860s many were forced to admit that these expectations were overly optimistic. The asylum population grew, but the cures were not effected. Overcrowding resulted; more asylums were built. "No sooner were new accommodations created than they were occupied, and there was nearly always a backlog of patients in the workhouses or at home who could not obtain admission."[10] Individual treatment gave way under such pressure and custodial care resulted.

> Explicit definitions of the term incurable are hard to find, however; by and large the term is used as a synonym for the contemporary expression "long term patient." The 1854 Report describes an incurable as one who has been resident in an asylum for two years or more.[11]

Even by midcentury, asylums were in the paradoxical situation of not being able to cure because of the large number of incurables.

> These places are, we regret to say, filled with incurable patients and are thus rendered incapable of receiving those whose malady might admit cure. It has been the practice, in numerous instances, to detain the insane pauper at the workhouse or elsewhere, until he becomes dangerous or unmanageable, and then when his disease is beyond all medical relief to send him to a Lunatic Asylum where he may remain the rest of his life, a pensioner on the public. This practice which has been carried on for the sake of saving, in the first instance, to each Parish some small expense, has confirmed the malady of many poor persons, has destroyed the comfort of families, has ultimately imposed a heavy burden upon Parishes and counties, and has, in great measure nullified the utility of Public Lunatic Asylums, by converting them into a permanent refuge for the insane, instead of hospitals for their relief and care.[12]

Asylums were impeded in the proper execution of their task by the unexpected and growing numbers of incurable patients.[13]

It appears that the optimistic "potential for cure" based on that change in the psychological paradigm early in the century caused the institutional machinery to be put into place and then became its own undoing. The commissioners were probably correct in assuming that large numbers of insane were not identified until the facilities were available to house them. Optimism oiled the governmental machinery that ground out investigations, reports, legislation, and the subsequent bureaucratic implementation of asylum proliferation. Society ventured into unknown territory and became mired in this previously unexplored area. Can we judge this society retrospectively? Must we construct unsubstantiated theories of social control to explain this failure of optimism?

> What those with an affinity for the "social Control" mode of explanation have done is to confuse the by-product with the intention. In addition, these scholars also fail to recognize that it is not social control in general that they are rejecting, but specific forms of control with which they disagree. From a purely logical point of view, the very definition of society presupposes the existence of controls. Indeed, only an absolute anarchist rejects the very idea of any social controls.[14]

There is nothing new in the assumption of a controlling elite:

> Neither is there anything particularly new in observing that those who have power, authority and influence seek to use these to protect and preserve the state of things which gives them power, and to maintain the peaceful, and preferably contented, subordination of those less comfortable than themselves. What is new is that in the last decade many social historians (often sociologists) have approached a whole range of the activities of power-groups as exercises in devising mechanisms of social control which conditioned and manipulated the propertyless masses into accepting and operating the forms and functions of behavior necessary to sustain the social order of an industrial society.[15]

Why has the last decade experienced the prevalence of this theory? An exchange of views between Michel Foucault and Lawrence Stone in a recent edition of *The New York Review of Books* may provide an answer. Foucault had objected to a review of a new edition of *Madness and Civilization* by Lawrence Stone. In a response to Foucault's objections, Stone suggested that:

> Foucault's generalizations lend themselves so easily to adaptation and extension, and perhaps distortion, by others. Thus his remarks about "the Doctor as an alienating figure" gave support and encouragement to others, like R. D. Laing in Britain and Thomas Szasz in America, to press their belief that institutional psychiatry is largely a conspiracy for power and prestige by a professional group with very dubious scientific credentials. Foucault certainly never sank to such mundane sociological explanations, but his writings led logically to it.[16]

Andrew Scull obviously followed Szasz in that belief and wrote in that tenor. Scull too has followers who write in the social control mode. Elaine Showalter, for example, in writing on *Victorian*

Women and Insanity,[17] utilized no statistical evidence and few historical sources and referred frequently to Scull for justification.[18]

What is troubling in all this is that the past is often turned to for justification of present policy decisions.

> Influenced by the opponents of institutionalization [social control theorists], a number of state legislatures during the 1960s and 1970s passed laws the goal of which, at least in theory, was to discharge as many involuntarily committed patients as possible from mental hospitals and thereby restore to them their rightful liberties.[19]

Like Gerald Grob, "I am pleased that those involved in policy decisions do turn to the past. What troubles me, however, is the quality of the historical data used in legitimating or opposing particular policies."[20]

Historical research does not tell us how psychiatry should be, or should have been, practiced; only how it has been practiced. The present study is an attempt to clarify the quantitative and qualitative historical data currently being used as the basis for policy decisions regarding the institutionalization of the mentally ill.

NOTES

Chapter 1. Introduction

1. United Kingdom, *Hansard's Parliamentary Debates* (hereafter *Hansard*), (Commons, 1st ser., vol. 8 (1806–7), c.514.

2. United Kingdom, Report of the Metropolitan Committee in Lunacy, 1844, British Parliamentary Papers (hereafter BPP), sess. 621, Irish University Press Series of British Parliamentary Papers (hereafter IUP), vol. 18, p. 1.

3. *Report of the Metropolitan Committee in Lunacy, Together With Minutes of Evidence, 1890* (London: C. J. G. & F. Rivington), p. 12.

4. Michel Foucault, *Madness and Civilization: A History of Insanity in the Age of Reason* (New York: Random House, 1965), p. 39.

5. George Rosen, *Madness in Society: Chapters in the Historical Sociology of Mental Illness* (Chicago: University of Chicago Press, 1968).

6. Ibid., p. ix.

7. Ibid., p. 180.

8. Thomas S. Szasz, *The Manufacture of Madness* (New York: Harper and Row, 1970).

9. Ibid., p. 160.

10. Ibid., p. xxv.

11. Andrew T. Scull, *Museums of Madness: The Social Organization of Insanity in Nineteenth-Century England* (New York: St. Martin's Press, 1979).

12. Ibid., p. 14.

13. Ibid., p. 15.

14. Ibid., p. 14.

15. Ibid., pp. 240, 250.

16. The most complete work on private asylums is William Parry-Jones, *The Trade in Lunacy: A Study of Private Madhouses in England in the Eighteenth and Nineteenth Centuries* (London: Routledge & Kegan Paul, 1972).

17. See Ruth G. Hodgkinson, *The Origins of the National Health Service: The Medical Services of the New Poor Law, 1834–1871* (Berkeley: University of California Press, 1967), pp. 176–85; 575–92.

18. See Patricia H. Allderidge, *Historical Notes on the Bethlem Royal Hospital* (Beckenham, Kent: Bethlem Archives, 1971).

19. It was not unusual for the government to appropriate space in private asylums for the care of pauper (government-supported) lunatics, prior to the erection of county asylums. The act of 1845 greatly modified this practice, subsequently swelling the number of pauper lunatics accounted for in county asylums.

20. County of Essex, *Report of the Committee of Visitors for the County of Essex Asylum* (Chelmsford: January 1854), p. 2.

21. Ibid., p. 5.

22. Allderidge, *Notes on Bethlem Hospital*, p. 1.

23. Ibid., p. 2.

24. Ibid., p. 3.

25. In 1853, Bethlem was considered a registered hospital under the jurisdiction of the commissioners in lunacy.

26. Alldridge, *Notes on Bethlem Hospital*, p. 5.

27. IUP, *Mental Health*, 6 (Shannon, Ireland: Irish University Press, 1968–70), p. 165.

Chapter 2. Development of the Asylum: Within the Social Service Delivery System

1. 22 Henry VIII, c.12, 1531.

2. Ibid.

3. Ibid.

4. Ibid.

5. 27 Henry VIII, c.25, 1536.

6. 5 Elizabeth, c.3, 1563.

7. 14 Elizabeth, c.5, 1572.

8. 18 Elizabeth, c.3, 1576.

9. Ibid.

10. 39 Elizabeth, c.3, 1597–98.

11. 43 Elizabeth, c.2, 1601.

12. 12 Anne, c.23, 1714.

13. 17 George II, c.5, 1744.

14. Parry-Jones, *The Trade in Lunacy*.

15. Ibid., p. 131.

16. Daniel Defoe, *A Review of the State of the English Nation* (London: Roberts and Company, 1706).

17. 14 George III, c.49, 1774.

18. 26 George III, c.91, 1786.

19. Select Committee Report of 1807, *Hansard*, 1st sec., vol. 8, c.516.

20. J. W. Rogers, *A Statement of the Cruelties, and Frauds which are practised in Mad-houses* (London, 1816), p. 23.

21. Select Committee Report of 1807, *Hansard*, 1st ser., vol. 8, c.516.

22. Ibid.

23. 48 George III, c.96, 1808.

24. 55 George III, c.46, 1815.

25. Parry-Jones, *Trade in Lunacy*, p. 15.

26. 9 George IV, c.41, 1828.

27. Karl deSchweinitz, *England's Road to Social Security* (New York: A. S. Barnes, 1943).

28. For an interesting summary of the transition, see Mark Blaug, "The Myth of the Old Poor Law and the Making of the New," *The Journal of Economic History* 23, no. 2 (June 1963): 151–84.

29. 4 & 5 William IV, c.76, 1834.

30. deSchweinitz, *Road to Social Security*, pp. 129–30.

31. Report of the 1838 Select Committee, *Hansard*, 3d ser., vol. 42 (1838), v. 1170.

32. Report of Assistant Commissioner Charles Mott, First Annual Report of the Poor Law Commissioners, 1838, BPP sess. 500, vol. 35, p. 156.

33. Ruth G. Hodgkinson, *The Origins of the National Health Service* (Berkeley: University of California Press, 1969), p. 578.

34. Report of the 1838 Select Committee on the Further Amendment of the Poor Law Act, *Hansard*, 3d ser., vol 42, c.1171.

35. Hodgkinson, *Origins of National Health Service*, p. 183.

36. Annual Report of the Metropolitan Commissioners in Lunacy, 1838, BPP, IUP, sess. 56, vol. 6, p. 247.

37. Ibid.

38. 5 & 6 Victoria, c.57, 1842.

39. Report of the Metropolitan Commissioners in Lunacy, 1844, BPP, IUP, sess. 621, vol. 18, p. 5.

40. Ibid., p.21.

41. *Hansard*, 3d ser., vol. 81, 6 June 1845, c.194.

42. Ibid.

43. 8 & 9 Victoria, c.100, 1845.

44. Ibid.

45. Ibid.

46. Ibid.

47. 8 & 9 Victoria, c.126, 1845.

48. Ibid.

49. Ibid.

50. Ibid.

51. Ibid.

52. 8 & 9 Victoria, c.126, 1845.

53. 16 & 17 Victoria, c.70, 1853.

54. 8 & 9 Victoria, c.100, 1845.

55. Metropolitan Committee in Lunacy, *Hansard*, 3d ser., vol. 18 (1844), p. 26.

56. *Hansard*, 2d ser., 1828, vol. 18, c.583–84.

57. Ibid.

58. A detailed discussion of this subject is taken up in chapter 6 of this study.

Chapter 3. The Development of the Health-Care Delivery System: The Medical Profession

1. The Medical Practitioners' Bill, *Hansard*, 3d ser., vol. 150 (1858), c.1406.

2. *Hansard*, 3d ser., vol. 150, 1858, c.1411.

3. Ibid., c.1410.

4. Ibid., c.1412.

5. Ibid.

6. Ibid.

7. Ibid., c.1413.

8. Ibid.

9. Ibid.

10. Ibid.

11. Ibid., c.1414.

12. Ibid., c.1406

13. F. N. L. Poynter, *The Evolution of Medical Education in Britain* (Baltimore: William Wilkins Company, 1966), p. 20.

14. Ibid., p. 23.

15. Brian Abel-Smith, *The Hospitals in England and Wales* (Cambridge: Harvard University Press, 1964), p. 2.

16. IUP, *The Medical Profession*, vol. 1, p. 5.

17. Ibid., pp. 5–6.

18. On the evolution of the surgeons in Britain, see Poynter, *Medical Education in Britain*.

19. S. Kramer, *The English Craft Guilds* (New York: Columbia University Press, 1927), p. 18.

20. Frederick F. Cartwright, *A Social History of Medicine* (London: Longman Group Limited, 1977), p. 45.

21. *Hansard*, 2d ser., 1827, volume 17, c.1346–48.

22. Thomas Wakley, ed., *The Lancet* 9 (October 1825): 5.

23. Ibid., p. 9.

24. The Apothecary Act of 1815 will be discussed at length later in this chapter.

25. Poynter, *Medical Education in Britain*, p. 71.

26. *Hansard*, 2d ser., 1827, vol. 17, c.1346.

27. Ibid.

28. Poynter, *Medical Education in Britain*, p. 78.

29. Ibid., p. 61.

30. Ibid., p. 65.

31. *Hansard*, 2d ser., 1827, vol. 17, c.1346.

32. Ibid.

33. Ibid., c.1346–47.

34. IUP, *Medical Profession*, vol. 2, pp. 7–9.

35. Ibid., p. 111.

36. Ibid.

37. *Hansard*, 2d ser., 1828, vol. 18, c.584.

38. M. W. Flinn, ed., Introduction to *Report on the Sanitary Condition of the Labouring Population of Great Britain* (Edinburgh: University of Edinburgh Press, 1965), pp. 34–35.

39. Abel-Smith, *Hospitals in England and Wales*, p. 17.

40. IUP, *Medical Profession*, vol. 1, p. 5.

41. Frederick Cartwright, *A Social History of Medicine* (London: Longman Group Ltd., 1977), p. 105.

42. Wakley, *The Lancet*, p. 4.

43. ibid., p. 5.

44. Ibid., pp. 4–5.

45. Ibid.

46. Ibid., p. 14.

47. Ibid., p. 17.

48. Poynter, *Medical Education in Britain*, p. 137.

49. *Lancet*, p. 17

50. Poynter, *Medical Education in Britain* p. 121.

51. Erwin H. Ackerknecht, *History and Geography of Diseases* (New York: Hafner Publishing Co., Inc., 1972), p. 24.

52. Cartwright, *Social History of Medicine*, p. 99.

53. Ibid.

54. Ackerknecht, *History and Geography of Diseases*, p. 26.

55. Edwin Chadwick, *Report From London and Berkshire: Extracts from the Information received by His Majesty's Commission as to the Administration and Operation of the Poor Laws* (1833), p. 316.

56. Ackerknecht, *History and Geography of Disease*, pp. 22–31.

57. For details on prevention, see *Snow on Cholera*, a reprint of two papers by John Snow (New York: The Commonwealth Fund, 1936).

58. Ackerknecht, *History and Geography of Disease*, pp. 32–47.

59. Richard Millar, *Clinical Lectures on the Contagious Typhus Epidemics in Glasgow and the Vicinity* (Glasgow, 1833), p. 11.

60. Ibid., p. 14.

61. Edwin Chadwick, *Report on the Sanitary Condition of the Labouring Population of Great Britain, 1842*, ed. M. W. Flinn (Edinburgh: Edinburgh University Press, 1965).

62. For the career of Dr. Duncan, see W. M. Frazer, *Duncan of Liverpool* (London: Wilson Co., 1947).

63. Chadwick, *Sanitary Report*, p. 422.

64. *The Times*, 29 August 1842; *The Morning Chronicle*, 30 August 1842.

65. *The Quarterly Review* 71 (March 1843): 417–53.

66. G. M. Young, *Victorian England: Portrait of an Age* (London: Oxford University Press, 1949), p. 11.

67. General Medical Order, Article III, issued by the Poor Law Commission Office, Somerset House, 12 March 1842.

68. Hodgkinson, *Origins of the National Service*, p. 295.

69. Ibid., p. 269.

70. 21 & 22 Victoria, c. 89, 90, 1858.

71. Ibid.

72. Poynter, *Medical Education in Britain*, p. 197.

73. Thomas Szasz, *The Myth of Mental Illness: Foundations of a Theory of Personal Conduct* (New York: Harper, 1961), p. 17.

74. Szasz, *The Manufacture of Madness*, p. 143.

75. Martin Roth, "Schizophrenia and the Theories of Thomas Szasz," *British Journal of Psychiatry* 129 (1976): 307–26.

76. Ibid., p. 318.

Chapter 4. The Growth of Science and the Change in the Psychological Paradigm

1. Thomas S. Kuhn, *The Structure of Scientific Revolutions*, 2d ed. (London: University of Chicago Press, 1970), pp. 43–51.

2. Ibid.

3. Ibid.

4. Ibid., p. 77.

5. Ibid., pp. 43–51.

6. Ibid., pp. 91–109.

7. Thomas H. Leahey, *A History of Psychology* (Englewood Cliffs, N.J.: Prentice-Hall, 1980), p. 92.

8. Ibid., p. 102.

9. David Hume, *An Enquiry Concerning Human Understanding* (Indianapolis: Hackett Publishing Co., 1977), pp. 10–11.

10. Ibid., p. 14.

11. Ibid., p. 57.

12. Leahey, *History of Psychology*, p. 143.

13. William L. Reese, *Dictionary of Philosophy and Religion* (Sussex, England: Harvester Press, 1980), p. 53.

14. William S. Sahakian, *History of Philosophy* (New York: Barnes and Noble, 1968), pp. 242–43.

15. Leahey, *History of Psychology*, p. 147.

16. William F. Bynum, Jr., "Rationales for Therapy in British Psychiatry, 1780–1835," *Medical History* 3 (1974): 16.

17. Ibid.

18. Andrew Scull, "Moral Treatment Reconsidered: Some Sociological Comments on an Episode in the History of British Psychiatry," *Psychological Medicine* 2 (1974): 3.

19. Roger Cooter, "Phrenology and the British Alienists, 1825–1845," *Medical History* 7 (1976): 3.

20. L. S. Hearnshaw, *A Short History of British Psychiatry* (New York: Barnes and Noble, 1964), pp. 18–19.

21. K. M. Dallenbach, "The History and Derivation of the Word 'Function' as a Systematic Term in Psychology," *American Journal of Psychiatry* 26 (1915): 484.

22. Leahey, *History of Psychology,* p. 160.

23. Hearnshaw, *British Psychiatry,* p. 20.

24. Cooter, "Phrenology," p. 6.

25. Ibid., p. 8.

26. E. H. Ackerknecht, *Medicine at the Paris Hospital* (Baltimore: Johns Hopkins Press, 1967), p. 172.

27. Hearnshaw, *British Psychiatry,* p. 20.

28. Ibid., p. 22.

29. Kuhn, *Scientific Revolutions,* pp. 43–51.

Chapter 5. The Myth of Moral Management and the Great Unwanted

1. Andrew Scull, ed., *Madhouses, Mad-Doctors, and Madmen* (Philadelphia: University of Pennsylvania Press, 1981), p. 111.

2. Foucault, *Madness and Civilization,* pp. 163–64.

3. Ibid., p. 166.

4. Ibid., p. 172.

5. John Conolly, *The Treatment of the Insane before and after the Advent of Moral Management* (London: Smith, Elder & Co., 1856), p. 36.

6. Foucault, *Madness and Civilization,* p. 185.

7. Conolly, *Treatment of the Insane,* pp. 12–16.

8. P. H. Pinel, *A Treatise on Insanity* (New York: Hafner Publishing, 1962; a facsimile of the London 1806 edition), p. 48.

9. E. Esquirol, *Mental Maladies: Treatise on Insanity* (Philadelphia: Lee and Blanchard, 1845), pp. 72–73.

10. Daniel Hack Tuke, *Reform in the Treatment of the Insane* (London: John Churchill Company, 1892), p. 34.

11. Ibid.

12. Ibid., p. 38.

13. William Willis Moseley, *Eleven Chapters on Nervous and Mental Complaints* (London: Simpkin, Marshall & Co., 1838), p. 129.

14. Ibid.

15. Ibid., p. 130.

16. Robert Gardiner Hill, *Total Abolition of Personal Restraint in the Treatment of the Insane* (London: Simpkin, Marshall, 1839), p. 39.

17. Vieda Skultans, *English Madness* (London: Routledge & Kegan Paul, 1979), p. 65.

18. John Conolly, *The Treatment of the Insane without Mechanical Restraints* (London: Smith, Elder and Co., 1857), p. 59.

19. Ibid., p. 61.

20. Scull, *Madhouses*, p. 52.

21. Skultans, *English Madness*, p. 105.

22. F. M. L. Thompson, "Social Control in Victorian Britain," *The Economic History Review* 34, no. 2 (1981): 190.

23. Scull, *Museums of Madness*, p. 240.

24. Ibid., p. 250.

25. Details of these hospital selections and the parameters of year selection will be found in chapter 1 of this study.

26. Kenneth J. Bowman and Matthew Cahill, eds., *SPSS Primer, Statistical Package for the Social Sciences* (New York: McGraw-Hill, 1975), p. 65.

27. Ibid., p. 70.

28. The validity of these comparative statistics is measured by the chi-square test for statistical significance. This test shows the probability that the observed joint distribution of cases would have happened by chance when no association existed between the two variables in the population. The chi square tests the general distribution of a table. The statistic produced is said to be statistically significant at a certain user-chosen level. Social scientists typically accept as statistically significant those relationships that have only an .05, .01, or .001 probability of occurring by chance. For the purpose of this study a .05 level will be used to indicate statistical significance.

29. D. R. Mitchell, *European Historical Statistics 1750–1970* (London: Macmillan, 1975), p. 8.

30. Edward Jarvis, "On the Comparative Liability of Males and Females to Insanity, and Their Comparative Curability and Mortality When Insane," *American Journal of Insanity* 7 (1850): 142–71. Jarvis studies 250 hospitals in the United States and Europe and found men more prone to mental disorder than women based on their representation in the inmate population.

31. Bruce P. Dohrenwend and Barbara Snell Dohrenwend, *Social Status and Psychological Disorder: A Causal Inquiry* (New York: Wiley-Interscience, 1969).

32. David Roberts, "The Paterfamilias of the Victorian Governing Classes," in *The Victorian Family*, ed. Anthony S. Wohl (London: Croom Helm, 1978), p. 60. Roberts found the average number of children in families of the peerage between 1800 and 1850 to be 4.5.

33. This pattern of ideographic notation was devised by Peter Laslett to depict family structures in various societies and appears in *Household and Family in Past Time* (Cambridge: Cambridge University Press, 1972); the key appears on p. 41.

34. Ibid., p. 49.

35. The "admitting authority" is the person or court who signed the patient into the asylum. In this study the admitting authority was found to be either the spouse, son or daughter, parent, sibling, in-law, respected community member (reverend, physician, or gentleman), Her Majesty, or the secretary of state. Until 1862 it was unlawful for a patient to commit himself.

36. Evidence is not available for the study years on actual availability of employment in the breakdown categories.

37. For a review of the five-class breakdown, see *Class, Status and Power*, ed. R. Bendix and S. Lipset. (New York: Free Press, 1953).

38. Bernard J. Gallagher, *The Sociology of Mental Illness*, (Englewood Cliffs, N.J.: Prentice-Hall, 1980) p. 251.

39. Ibid.

40. Ibid., p. 252.

41. Dohrenwend and Dohrenwend, *Social Status*, pp. 71–72.

42. David Mechanic, "Social Class and Schizophrenia," *Social Forces* 50 (1972): 305–29.

43. Gallagher, *Sociology of Mental Illness,* p. 253.

44. Ibid.

45. E. H. Hare, J. S. Price, and E. Slater, "Parental Social Class in Psychiatric Patients," *British Journal of Psychiatry* 121 (1972): 505–31.

46. Gallagher, *Sociology of Mental Illness,* p. 254.

47. More will be said on this subject later in this chapter, and the whole question of the validity of the social control theory will be discussed at length in the conclusion.

48. Scull, *Museums of Madness,* p. 242.

49. Gallagher, *Sociology of Mental Illness,* p. 12.

50. This researcher has not been able to find a reasonable explanation for this exception.

51. Gallagher, *Sociology of Mental Illness,* p. 92.

52. Ibid.

53. Melvin Kohn, "Social Class and Schizophrenia," *Schizophrenia Bulletin* 7 (1973): 60–79.

54. Ibid.

55. P. Keilholz, "Diagnosis and Therapy of the Depressive States," *Docum. Geigy Acta Psychosom.* 1 (1959): 62–89.

56. Ibid.

57. Robert N. Butler, "Thoughts on Aging," *American Journal of Psychiatry* (suppl.) 135 (1978): 14–16.

58. Ernest Becker, "Social Science and Psychiatry," *The Antioch Review* 23 (1963): 353.

59. A more detailed discussion of the social control theorists' constructs will be presented in the conclusion.

60. Scull, *Madhouses,* p. 111.

61. Janet Roebuck, *Urban Development in 19th-Century London* (London: Phillimore, 1979), p. 159.

Chapter 6. The Development of Centralized Bureaucracy: The Growth of Government Debate—An Alternate Theory

1. George Watson, *The English Ideology* (London: Allen Lane, 1973), p. 70.

2. Oliver MacDonagh, "The Nineteenth-Century Revolution in Government: A Reappraisal," *The Historical Journal* 1, no. 1 (1958): 52–67.

3. H. Simon, D. Smithburg, and V. Thompson, *Public Administration* (New York: Alfred Knopf, 1950), p. 428.

4. K. B. Smellie, *One Hundred Years of English Government* (London: Macmillan, 1950), p. 331.

5. A. V. Dicey, *Law and Opinion in England* (London: Macmillan, 1919), p. 10.

6. Ibid., p. 62.

7. Ibid.

8. Ibid., p. 63.

9. Ibid., p. 64.

10. Ibid., p. 69.

11. This aspect of the dispute will be discussed at length later in the chapter.

12. G. R. Elton, *The Tudor Revolution in Government* (Cambridge: Cambridge University Press, 1953).

13. MacDonagh, "Revolution in Government," pp. 52–53.

14. Ibid., p. 55.

15. Ibid., pp. 52–57.

16. Ibid., p. 58.

17. Ibid., p. 59.

18. Ibid., p. 60.

19. Ibid.

20. Ibid.

21. Simon, Smithburg, and Thompson, *Public Administration,* pp. 297–98.

22. Henry Parris, "The Nineteenth-Century Revolution in Government: A Reappraisal Reappraised," *The Historical Journal* 3, no. 1 (1960): 17–37.

23. Ibid., p. 18.

24. To be taken up later in the chapter with the discussion concerning utilitarianism and laissez-faire.

25. Parris, "Revolution Reappraised," p. 18.

26. Ibid., p. 17.

27. Ibid., p. 23.

28. Ibid., pp. 19, 23.

29. Ibid., p. 18.

30. Ibid., pp. 26–27.

31. Ibid., p. 33.

32. Ibid.

33. Ibid., p. 36.

34. Ibid., p. 37.

35. Jenifer Hart, "Nineteenth-Century Social Reform: A Tory Interpretation of History," *Past and Present* 31 (1965): 76.

36. Ibid., p. 39.

37. D. Roberts, "Jeremy Bentham and the Victorian Administrative State," *Victorian Studies* 2, no. 3 (1959); 245–66.

38. Hart, "Tory Interpretation," p. 45.

39. Ibid., p. 47.

40. Arthur J. Taylor, *Laissez-faire and State Intervention in Nineteenth-Century Britain* (London: Macmillan, 1972).

41. Ibid., p. 11.

42. Ibid.

43. Ibid., p. 12.

44. Dicey, *Law and Opinion,* p. 147.

45. J. M. Keynes, *The End of Laissez-faire* (New York: Macmillan, 1926), p. 18.

46. C. R. Fay, *Great Britain from Adam Smith to the Present Day* (Cambridge: Cambridge University Press, 1928), p. 367.

47. Taylor, *Laissez-faire and State Intervention,* pp. 32–33.

48. J. B. Brebner, "Laissez-faire and State Intervention in Nineteenth-Century Britain," *Journal of Economic History* 8 (1948): 61.

49. Taylor, *Laissez-faire,* p. 34.

50. Dicey, *Law and Opinion,* pp. 303–10.

51. Taylor, *Laissez-faire,* p. 34.

52. Ibid., p. 36.

53. David Roberts, *The Victorian Origins of the British Welfare State* (New Haven: Yale University Press, 1960).

54. Ibid., p. 326.

55. Phyllis Deane, *The First Industrial Revolution* (Cambridge: Cambridge University Press, 1965), pp. 214–15.

56. Ibid., p.215.

57. Taylor, *Laissez-faire*, p. 49.

58. 42 George III, c.73, 1802.

59. Oliver MacDonagh, *Early Victorian Government 1830–1870* (London: Weidenfeld and Nicolson, 1977), p. 22.

60. Ibid., p. 23.

61. Ibid., p. 32.

62. Report of the Select Committee on Factory Children's Labour, 1831–1832, xv (evidence of Thomas Bennett), *Hansard*, 3d ser., vol. 21, c.706–8.

63. MacDonagh, *Early Victorian Government*, p. 33.

64. Ibid., p. 43.

65. Harold J. Schultz, *History of England* (London: Barnes & Noble, 1971), p. 218.

66. MacDonagh, *Early Victorian Government*, p. 78.

67. Ibid., p. 79.

68. *Hansard*, 3d, ser., vol. 39 (1840), c.196.

69. Ibid., c. 1336–37.

70. MacDonagh, *Early Victorian Government*, p. 80.

71. 5 & 6 Victoria, c.99, 1842.

72. Ibid.

73. MacDonagh, *Early Victorian Government*, p. 82.

74. Ibid.

75. *Hansard*, 3d, ser., vol. 12 (1843), c.1076.

76. MacDonagh, *Early Victorian Government*, p. 87.

77. 13 & 14 Victoria, c.100, 1850.

78. Ibid.

79. MacDonagh, *Early Victorian Government*, p. 89.

80. Ibid., p. 93.

81. Reports of Mine Inspectors quoted in MacDonagh, *Early Victorian Government*, pp. 93–94.

82. Ibid.

83. Hew Strachan, "The Early Victorian Army and the Nineteenth-Century Revolution in Government," *The English Historical Review* 95, no. 377 (1980): 782–809.

84. Ibid., p.785.

85. Ibid., p. 786.

86. Ibid., p. 783.

87. Ibid., p. 784.

88. Ibid.

Chapter 7. Conclusion

1. For an excellent summary of this subject, see James E. O'Neill, "Finding a Policy for the Sick Poor," *Victorian Studies* 7, no. 3 (March 1964): 273–97.

2. House of Commons Select Committee Report of 1807, BPP, IUP, vol. 18, p. 121.

3. 1844 Report of the Metropolitan Committee in Lunacy, BPP, IUP, vol. 18, p. 148.

4. 1890 Report of the Metropolitan Committee in Lunacy (London: Rivington), p. 16.

5. Scull, *Museums of Madness*, p. 226.

6. Commissioners in Lunacy Annual Report, 1861, BPP, IUP, vol. 18, p. 77.

7. Scull, *Museums of Madness*, p. 242.

8. John K. Walton, "Lunacy in the Industrial Revolution: A Study of Asylum Admissions in Lancashire, 1848–1850," *Journal of Social History* 13, no. 1 (Fall 1979): 17.

9. Peter McCandless, "Build! Build! The Controversy Over the Care of the Chronically Insane in England 1855–1870," *Bulletin of the History of Medicine* 12 (1979): 353–54.

10. Ibid., p. 354.

11. Skultans, *English Madness*, p. 116.

12. Select Committee Report of 1854, quoted in Skultans, *English Madness*, p. 115.

13. Skultans, *English Madness*, p. 115.

14. Gerald N. Grob, "Rediscovering Asylums: The Unhistorical History of the Mental Hospital," in *The Therapeutic Revolution: Essays in the Social History of American Medicine*, ed. Morris J. Vogel and Charles E. Rosenberg (Philadelphia: University of Pennsylvania Press, 1979), p. 149.

15. F. M. L. Thompson, "Social Control in Victorian Britain," *Economic History Review* 4, no. 2 (May 1981): 189.

16. Lawrence Stone and Michel Foucault, "An Exchange," *New York Review of Books* 30, no. 5 (31 March 1983): 10, 43.

17. Elaine Showalter, "Victorian Women and Insanity," *Victorian Studies*, 23, no. 2 (Winter 1980): 157–81.

18. Michel Foucault, *The History of Sexuality: An Introduction* (New York: Vintage Press, 1980), 1: 123. In this later work, Foucault clarifies his position with regard to sexuality: "[The] deployment of sexuality was first established as a new distribution of pleasures, discourses, truths and powers; it has to be seen as the self-affirmation of one class rather than the enslavement of another; a defense, a protection, a strengthening, and an exaltation that were eventually extended to others—at the cost of different transformations—as a means of social control and political subjugation."

19. Grob, "Rediscovering Asylums," p. 143.

20. Ibid., p. 135.

REFERENCES

Primary Sources

Local Government and Hospital Reports

Bethlehem Hospital. *Admission Records*. London, 1845–62.

County of Essex. *Report of the Committee of Visitors for the County of Essex Asylum*. Chelmsford, January 1854.

Essex County Asylum. *Admissions Records*. Colchester, 1845–62.

Essex Lunatic Asylum Report of the Committee of Visitors, Report of the Medical Superintendent and Other Papers Relating to the Asylum. Chelmsford: Meggy and Chalk Printers, 1854, 1857, 1859, 1860, 1861, 1866, 1867.

General Report of the Royal Hospitals of Bridewell and Bethlem for the Year Ending 31st December. London: David Batten, Printer, 1851, 1852, 1853, 1854, 1855, 1856, 1857, 1858, 1859, 1860.

Haydock Lodge Asylum. *Admissions Records*. Lancashire, 1845–62.

Haydock Lodge Lunatic Asylum. Advertisement circular printed 1845.

Hereford Asylum. *Register of Insane Persons Received into and Discharged from Hereford Asylum*. Hereford, 1836–38.

———. *Medical Certificates*. Hereford, 1836–1838.

———. *Statement and Order of Medical Certificates Authorizing the Reception of an Insane Person to Hereford Asylum*. Hereford, 1836–38.

London Metropolitan Committee in Lunacy. *Report together with Minutes of Evidence*, 1844, 1890.

Secondary Sources

Major Sources Consulted

Allderidge, Patricia H., ed. *The Bethlem Hospital Historical Museum Catalogue*. Beckenham, Kent: Bethlem Hospital Board of Governors, 1976.

———. *Historical Notes on the Bethlem Royal Hospital*. Beckenham, Kent: Bethlem Archives, 1971.

Brown, A. F. J. *Essex People 1750–1900*. Chelmsford: Essex County Council, 1972.

———. *Essex at Work 1700–1815*. Chelmsford: Essex County Council, 1969.

Dicey, A. V. *Law and Public Opinion in England*. London: Macmillan, 1919.

Flinn, M. W., ed. *Edwin Chadwick's Report on the Sanitary Condition of the Labouring Population of Great Britain*. Reprint: Edinburgh: University of Edinburgh Press, 1965.

Foucault, Michel. *Madness and Civilization*. New York: Random House, 1965.

Kuhn, Thomas S. *The Structure of Scientific Revolutions*. 2d ed. London: University of Chicago Press, 1970.

MacDonagh, Oliver. "The Nineteenth-Century Revolution in Government: A Reappraisal." *The Historical Journal* 1, no. 1 (1958): 52–67.

Parris, Henry. "The Nineteenth-Century Revolution in Government: A Reappraisal Reappraised." *The Historical Journal* 3, no. 1 (1960): 17–37.

Parry-Jones, William. *The Trade in Lunacy: A Study of Private Madhouse in England in the 18th and 19th Centuries*. London: Routledge & Kegan Paul, 1972.

Rosen, George. *Madness and Society: Chapters in the Historical Sociology of Mental Illness*. Chicago: University of Chicago Press, 1968.

Scull, Andrew T. *Museums of Madness: The Social Organization of Insanity in Nineteenth-Century England*. New York: Harper and Row, 1970.

Wakely, Thomas, ed. *The Lancet* 9 (October 1825).

Other Sources

Abel-Smith, Brian. *The Hospitals 1800–1948: A Study in Social Administration in England and Wales*. Cambridge: Harvard University Press, 1964.

Ackerknecht, E. H. *Medicine at the Paris Hospital*. Baltimore: Johns Hopkins Press, 1967.

————. *The History of Geography of the Most Important Diseases*. New York: Hafner Publishing, 1972.

Alexander, Marc. "The Administration of Madness in 19th Century Paris." Diss., Johns Hopkins University, 1976.

Anonymous. "Inside Bedlam by an Outsider." *Tinsley's Magazine* 3 (November 1868): 456–63.

Barker-Benfield, G. J. *The Horrors of the Half-Known Life*. New York: Harper and Row, 1976.

Battiscombe, Georgina. *Shaftesbury*. London: Constable and Co., 1974.

Becker, Ernest. "Social Science and Psychiatry." *The Antioch Review*. 23 (1963): 359–80.

Bendix, R., and S. Lipset, eds. *Class, Status and Power*. New York: Free Press, 1953.

Best, G. F. A. *Shaftesbury*. New York: Arco Publishing, 1964.

Blau, Peter M. *Bureaucracy in Modern Society*. New York: Random House, 1966.

————. *The Dynamics of Bureaucracy*. Chicago: University of Chicago Press, 1955.

Branca, Patricia. *Women in Europe since 1750*. London: Billings and Sons, 1978.

Brebner, J. B. "Laissez-faire and State Intervention in Nineteenth-Century Britain." *Journal of Economic History* 8 (1948): 61–84.

Brownowski, J. *Magic, Science, and Civilization*. New York: Columbia University Press, 1978.

Bowman, Kenneth, and Matthew Cahill, eds. *SPSS Primer: Statistical Package for the Social Sciences*. New York: McGraw-Hill, 1975.

Bullaugh, Vern L. *Sexual Variance in Society and History*. Chicago: University of Chicago Press, 1976.

Burn, Richard. *The History of the Poor Laws*. 1764. Reprint: New York: Augus tus M. Kelley, 1973.

Butler, Robert N. "Thoughts on Ageing." *American Journal of Psychiatry* 135, Suppl. (1978): 1–29.

Bynum, William F., Jr. "Rationales for Therapy in British Psychiatry, 1780–1835." *Medical History* 3 (1974): 6–27.

Cartwright, Frederick. *A Social History of Medicine*. London: Longman Group, 1977.

Chadwick, Edwin. *Report from London and Berkshire: Extracts from the Information Received by His Majesty's Commission as to the Administration and Operation of the Poor Laws*. London, 1833.

Chaplin, Arnold. *Medicine in England during the Reign of George III*. London: Henry Kimpton, 1919.

Coe, Rodney M., ed. *Sociology of Medicine*. New York: McGraw-Hill, 1970.

Conolly, John. *The Treatment of the Insane before and after the Advent of Moral Management*. London: Smith, Elder & Co., 1856.

———. *The Treatment of the Insane without Mechanical Restraints*. London: Smith, Elder & Co., 1857.

Cooter, Roger. "Phrenology and the British Alienists, 1825–1845." *Medical History* 7 (1976): 1–21.

Cromwell, Valerie. "Interpretations of Nineteenth-Century Administration: An Analysis." *Victorian Studies* 9, no. 3 (March 1966): 245–55.

Cullen, Michael J. *The Statistical Movement in Early Victorian Britain*. Sussex: Harvester Press, 1975.

Dallenbach, K. M. "The History and Derivation of the Word 'Function' as a Systematic Term in Psychology." *American Journal of Psychiatry* 26 (1915): 476–503.

Deane, Phyllis. *The First Industrial Revolution*. Cambridge: Cambridge University Press, 1965.

deSchweinitz, Karl. *England's Road to Social Security*. New York: A. S. Barnes & Company, 1943.

Dickens, Charles. *Hard Times*. New York: Norton, 1966.

Digby, Anne. *Pauper Palaces*. Boston: Routledge & Kegan Paul, 1978.

Dohrenwend, Bruce P., and Barbara Snell Dohrenward. *Social Status and Psychological Disorder: A Causal Inquiry*. New York: Wiley-Interscience, 1969.

Drake, Michael, ed. *Population in Industrialization*. London: Metheun, 1969.

Dye, Thomas R. *Understanding Public Policy*. Englewood Cliffs, N.J.: Prentice-Hall, 1975.

Elton, G. R. *The Tudor Revolution in Government*. Cambridge: Cambridge University Press, 1953.

Erickson, Carolly. *The Medieval Vision: Essays in History and Perception*. New York: Oxford University Press, 1976.

Esquirol, E. *Mental Maladies: Treatise on Insanity*. Philadelphia: Lea and Blanchard, 1845.

Fay, C. R. *Great Britain from Adam Smith to the Present Day*. Cambridge: Cambridge University Press, 1928.

Forster, Robert, and Orest Ranum, eds. *Deviants and the Abandoned in French Society: Selections from the Annales, Volume 4.* Baltimore: Johns Hopkins University Press, 1978.

———. *Medicine and Society in France: Selections from the Annales, Volume 6.* Baltimore: Johns Hopkins University Press, 1980.

———. *Biology of Man in History: Selections from the Annales.* Baltimore: Johns Hopkins University Press, 1975.

Foucault, Michel. *The History of Sexuality, 1.* New York: Vintage Press, 1980.

Frazer, W. M. *Duncan of Liverpool.* London: Wilson Co., 1947.

Gallagher, Bernard J. *The Sociology of Mental Illness.* Englewood Cliffs, N.J.: Prentice-Hall, 1980.

Gardiner Hill, Robert. *Total Abolition of Personal Restraint in the Treatment of the Insane.* London: Simpkin, Marshall & Co., 1839.

Haley, Bruce. *The Healthy Body and Victorian Culture.* Cambridge: Harvard University Press, 1978.

Hare, E. H., J. S. Price, and E. Slater. "Parental Social Class and Psychiatric Patients." *British Journal of Psychiatry* 121 (1972): 505–31.

Hart, Jenifer. "Nineteenth-Century Social Reform: A Tory Interpretation of History." *Past and Present* 31 (1965): 70–91.

Hearnshaw, L. S. *A Short History of British Psychology 1840–1940.* New York: Barnes and Noble, 1964.

Himmelfarb, Gertrude. *Victorian Minds.* New York: Alfred Knopf, 1968.

Hodgkinson, Ruth G. *The Origins of the National Health Service: The Medical Services of the New Poor Law, 1834–1871.* Berkeley: University of California Press, 1967.

Hunter, Richard, and Ida Macalpine. *George III and the Madbusiness.* New York: Pantheon, 1970.

———. *Psychiatry for the Poor: Colney Hatch Asylum-Hospital: A Medical and Social History.* London: Dawson's Press, 1974.

Jarvis, Edward. "On the Comparative Liability of Males and Females to Insanity, and their Comparative Curability and Mortality When Insane." *American Journal of Insanity* 7 (1850): 142–71.

———. *Insanity and Idiocy in Massachusetts: Report of the Commission on Lunacy, 1855.* Reprint: Cambridge: Harvard University Press, 1971.

Jones, Kathleen. *A History of Mental Health Services.* New York: Routledge, 1972.

———. *Mental Health and Social Policy.* London: Routledge & Kegan Paul, 1960.

Keilholz, P. "Diagnosis and Therapy of the Depressive States." *Docum. Geigy Acta Psychosom.* 1 (1959): 62–89.

Keynes, J. M. *The End of Laissez-faire.* New York: Macmillan, 1926.

Kohn, Melvin. "Social Class and Schizophrenia." *Schizophrenia Bulletin* 7 (1973): 60–79.

Kramer, S. *The English Craft Guilds.* New York: Columbia University Press, 1927.

La Polombara, Joseph, ed. *Bureaucracy and Political Development.* Princeton: Princeton University Press, 1963.

Laslet, Peter. *Household and Family in Past Time.* Cambridge: Cambridge University Press, 1972.

Lawton, Richard, ed. *The Census and Social Structure: An Interpretive Guide to the 19th Century Census for England and Wales.* London: Frank Cass & Co., 1978.

Leahey, Thomas H. *A History of Psychiatry.* Englewood Cliffs, N.J.: Prentice-Hall, 1980.

Mackay, Charles. *Extraordinary Popular Delusions and the Madness of Crowds.* New York: Harmony Books, 1980.

MacDonagh, Oliver. *Early Victorian Government 1830–1870.* London: Weidenfeld and Nicolson, 1977.

MacDonald, Michael. *Mystical Bedlam: Madness, Anxiety, and Healing in Seventeenth-Century England.* Cambridge: Cambridge University Press, 1981.

McCandless, Peter. "Liberty and Lunacy: The Victorians and Wrongful Confinement." *Journal of Social History* 11, no. 3 (Spring 1978): 366–85.

————. "Build! Build! The Controversy Over the Care of the Chronically Insane in England, 1855–1870." *The Bulletin of the History of Medicine* 2 (1979): 553–74.

Mechanic, David. "Social Class and Schizophrenia." *Social Forces* 50 (1972): 305–29.

Medeiras, James A., and David E. Schmitt. *Public Bureaucracy: Values and Perspectives.* North Scituate, Mass.: Duxbury Press, 1977.

Meyer, Marshall W. *Change in Public Bureaucracy.* Cambridge: Cambridge University Press, 1979.

Midelfort, Erik. "Madness and the Problems of Psychological History in the Sixteenth Century." *The Sixteenth Century Journal* 12, no. 1 (Spring 1981): 5–12.

Millar, Richard. *Clinical Lectures on the Contagious Typhus Epidemics in Glasgow and the Vicinity.* Glasgow: Knox Press, 1833.

Mitchell, B. R., and Phyllis Deane, eds. *Abstract of British Historical Statistics.* Cambridge: Cambridge University Press, 1962.

————. *Second Abstract of British Historical Statistics.* Cambridge: Cambridge University Press, 1971.

The Morning Chronicle [London], 30 August 1842.

Moseley, William Willis. *Eleven Chapters on Nervous and Mental Complaints.* London: Simpkin, Marshall & Co., 1838.

Mumford, Lewis. *Technics and Civilization.* New York: Harcourt Brace, 1962.

Nicholls, Sir George. *A History of the English Poor Law,* vol. 1. Reprint: New York: Augustus M. Kelley, 1967.

Nichols, Grandma. *The Great Nineteenth Century Medicine Manual.* Toronto: J. L. Nichols Co., 1894.

O'Neill, James E. "Finding a Policy for the Sick Poor." *Victorian Studies* 7, no. 3 (March 1964): 273–97.

Parris, Henry. *Constitutional Bureaucracy: The Development of British Central Administration Since the Eighteenth Century.* London: George Allen & Unwin, 1969.

Parsons, Talcott. *The Evolution of Societies.* Englewood Cliffs, N.J.: Prentice-Hall, 1977.

Peterson, Dale, ed. *A Mad People's History of Madness.* Pittsburgh: University of Pittsburgh Press, 1982.

Pinel, P. H. *A Treatise on Insanity 1806.* Reprint: New York: Hafner Publishing, 1962.

Poynter, F. N. L. *The Evolution of Medical Education in Britain.* Baltimore: William Wilkins, 1966.

The Quarterly Review 71 (March 1843).

Reimer, Eleanor S., and John C. Fout, eds., *European Women: A Documentary History 1789–1945*. New York: Schocken Books, 1980.

Roberts, David. "Jeremy Bentham and the Victorian Administrative State." *Victorian Studies* 2 (1959): 52–75.

———. *Victorian Origins of the British Welfare State*. New Haven: Yale University Press, 1960.

Roebuck, Janet. *Urban Development in 19th-Century London*. London: Phillimore & Co., 1979.

Rogers, J. W. *A Statement of the Cruelties and Frauds which are Practised in Madhouses*. London, 1816.

Roth, Martin. "Schizophrenia and the Theories of Thomas Szasz." *British Journal of Psychiatry* 129 (1976): 317–26.

Rothman, David J. *The Discovery of the Asylum*. Boston: Little Brown & Co., 1971.

Sahakian, William S. *History of Philosophy*. New York: Barnes and Noble, 1968.

Schultz, Harold J. *History of England*. London: Barnes and Noble, 1971.

Scull, Andrew T., ed. *Madhouses, Mad-Doctors and Madmen*. Philadelphia: University of Pennsylvania Press, 1981.

———. "Moral Treatment Reconsidered: Some Sociological Comments on an Episode in the History of British Psychiatry." *Psychological Medicine* 2 (1979): 1–33.

Showalter, Elaine. "Victorian Women and Insanity." *Victorian Studies* 23, no. 2 (Winter 1980): 157–81.

Simon, H., D. Smithburg, and V. Thompson. *Public Administration*. New York: Alfred Knopf, 1950.

Sisson, C. H. *The Spirit of British Administration*. London: Faber & Faber, 1959.

Skultans, Vieda. *Madness and Morals*. London: Routledge & Kegan Paul, 1975.

———. *English Madness*. London: Routledge & Kegan Paul, 1979.

Smellie, K. B. *One Hundred Years of English Government*. London: Macmillan, 1950.

Snow, John. *Snow on Cholera*. Reprint: London: Humphrey Milford, 1936.

Stack, John A. "The Juvenile Delinquent and the Revolution in Government 1825–1875." *The Historian* 42, no. 1 (November 1979): 42–57.

Stone, Lawrence, and Michel Foucault. "An Exchange." *New York Review of Books* 30, no. 5 (31 March 1983): 42–44.

Strachan, Hew. "The Early Victorian Army and the Nineteenth-Century Revolution in Government." *The English Historical Review* 95, no. 377 (October 1980): 782–809.

Szasz, Thomas S. *Law, Liberty and Psychiatry: An Inquiry into the Social Uses of Mental Health Practices*. London: Routledge & Kegan Paul, 1974.

———. *The Myth of Mental Illness: Foundations of a Theory of Personal Conduct*. New York: Harper, 1961.

Taylor, Arthur J. *Laissez-Faire and State Intervention in Nineteenth-Cetury Britain*. London: Macmillan, 1972.

Thompson, F. M. L. "Social Control in Victorian Britain." *The Economic History Review* 34, no. 2 (May 1981): 189–208.

Thompson, Victor A. *Without Sympathy or Enthusiasm*. Huntsville: University of Alabama Press, 1975.

The Times [London], 29 August 1842.

Tobias, J. J. *Crime and Police in England 1700–1900*. Dublin: Gill & MacMillan, 1979.

———. *Urban Crime in Victorian England*. New York: Schocken Books, 1972.

Trattner, Walter. *From Poor Law to Welfare State: A History of Social Welfare in America*. New York: MacMillan, 1974.

Tuke, Daniel Hack. *Reform in the Treatment of the Insane*. London: John Churchill Company, 1892.

Vogel, Morris J., and Charles Rosenberg, eds., *The Therapeutic Revolution: Essays in the Social History of American Medicine*. Philadelphia: University of Pennsylvania Press, 1979.

Wagar, Warren W. *World Views: A Study in Comparative History*. New York: Holt, Rinehart and Winston, 1977.

Walker, D. P. *Unclean Spirits: Possession and Exorcism in France and England in the Late 16th and Early 17thC*. Philadelphia: University of Pennsylvania Press, 1982.

Walton, John K. "Lunacy in the Industrial Revolution: A Study of Admissions in Lancashire, 1848–1850." *Journal of Social History* 13, no. 1 (Fall 1979): 1–21.

Watson, George. *The English Ideology: Studies in the Language of Victorian Politics*. London: Allen Lane, 1973.

Weber, Adna Ferrin. *The Growth of Cities in the Nineteenth Century: A Study in Statistics*. Ithaca, N.Y.: Cornell University Press, 1967.

Wohl, Anthony S., ed. *The Victorian Family*. London: Croom Helm, 1978.

Wrigley, E. A. *Population and History*. New York: McGraw-Hill, 1969.

———. *Nineteenth-Century Society: Essays in the Use of Quantitative Methods for the Study of Social Data*. Cambridge: Cambridge University Press, 1972.

Young, G. M. *Victorian England: Portrait of an Age*. London: Oxford University Press, 1949.

INDEX